Mometrix

TEST PREPARATION

NES®

Music

Secrets Study Guide

I0894301

DEAR FUTURE EXAM SUCCESS STORY

First of all, **THANK YOU** for purchasing Mometrix study materials!

Second, congratulations! You are one of the few determined test-takers who are committed to doing whatever it takes to excel on your exam. **You have come to the right place.** We developed these study materials with one goal in mind: to deliver you the information you need in a format that's concise and easy to use.

In addition to optimizing your guide for the content of the test, we've outlined our recommended steps for breaking down the preparation process into small, attainable goals so you can make sure you stay on track.

We've also analyzed the entire test-taking process, identifying the most common pitfalls and showing how you can overcome them and be ready for any curveball the test throws you.

Standardized testing is one of the biggest obstacles on your road to success, which only increases the importance of doing well in the high-pressure, high-stakes environment of test day. Your results on this test could have a significant impact on your future, and this guide provides the information and practical advice to help you achieve your full potential on test day.

Your success is our success

We would love to hear from you! If you would like to share the story of your exam success or if you have any questions or comments in regard to our products, please contact us at **800-673-8175** or **support@mometrix.com**.

Thanks again for your business and we wish you continued success!

Sincerely,
The Mometrix Test Preparation Team

Need more help? Check out our flashcards at:
http://MometrixFlashcards.com/NESINC

TABLE OF CONTENTS

Introduction

Thank you for purchasing this resource! You have made the choice to prepare yourself for a test that could have a huge impact on your future, and this guide is designed to help you be fully ready for test day. Obviously, it's important to have a solid understanding of the test material, but you also need to be prepared for the unique environment and stressors of the test, so that you can perform to the best of your abilities.

For this purpose, the first section that appears in this guide is the **Secret Keys**. We've devoted countless hours to meticulously researching what works and what doesn't, and we've boiled down our findings to the five most impactful steps you can take to improve your performance on the test. We start at the beginning with study planning and move through the preparation process, all the way to the testing strategies that will help you get the most out of what you know when you're finally sitting in front of the test.

We recommend that you start preparing for your test as far in advance as possible. However, if you've bought this guide as a last-minute study resource and only have a few days before your test, we recommend that you skip over the first two Secret Keys since they address a long-term study plan.

If you struggle with **test anxiety**, we strongly encourage you to check out our recommendations for how you can overcome it. Test anxiety is a formidable foe, but it can be beaten, and we want to make sure you have the tools you need to defeat it.

Secret Key #1 – Plan Big, Study Small

There's a lot riding on your performance. If you want to ace this test, you're going to need to keep your skills sharp and the material fresh in your mind. You need a plan that lets you review everything you need to know while still fitting in your schedule. We'll break this strategy down into three categories.

Information Organization

Start with the information you already have: the official test outline. From this, you can make a complete list of all the concepts you need to cover before the test. Organize these concepts into groups that can be studied together, and create a list of any related vocabulary you need to learn so you can brush up on any difficult terms. You'll want to keep this vocabulary list handy once you actually start studying since you may need to add to it along the way.

Time Management

Once you have your set of study concepts, decide how to spread them out over the time you have left before the test. Break your study plan into small, clear goals so you have a manageable task for each day and know exactly what you're doing. Then just focus on one small step at a time. When you manage your time this way, you don't need to spend hours at a time studying. Studying a small block of content for a short period each day helps you retain information better and avoid stressing over how much you have left to do. You can relax knowing that you have a plan to cover everything in time. In order for this strategy to be effective though, you have to start studying early and stick to your schedule. Avoid the exhaustion and futility that comes from last-minute cramming!

Study Environment

The environment you study in has a big impact on your learning. Studying in a coffee shop, while probably more enjoyable, is not likely to be as fruitful as studying in a quiet room. It's important to keep distractions to a minimum. You're only planning to study for a short block of time, so make the most of it. Don't pause to check your phone or get up to find a snack. It's also important to **avoid multitasking**. Research has consistently shown that multitasking will make your studying dramatically less effective. Your study area should also be comfortable and well-lit so you don't have the distraction of straining your eyes or sitting on an uncomfortable chair.

The time of day you study is also important. You want to be rested and alert. Don't wait until just before bedtime. Study when you'll be most likely to comprehend and remember. Even better, if you know what time of day your test will be, set that time aside for study. That way your brain will be used to working on that subject at that specific time and you'll have a better chance of recalling information.

Finally, it can be helpful to team up with others who are studying for the same test. Your actual studying should be done in as isolated an environment as possible, but the work of organizing the information and setting up the study plan can be divided up. In between study sessions, you can discuss with your teammates the concepts that you're all studying and quiz each other on the details. Just be sure that your teammates are as serious about the test as you are. If you find that your study time is being replaced with social time, you might need to find a new team.

Secret Key #2 – Make Your Studying Count

You're devoting a lot of time and effort to preparing for this test, so you want to be absolutely certain it will pay off. This means doing more than just reading the content and hoping you can remember it on test day. It's important to make every minute of study count. There are two main areas you can focus on to make your studying count.

Retention

It doesn't matter how much time you study if you can't remember the material. You need to make sure you are retaining the concepts. To check your retention of the information you're learning, try recalling it at later times with minimal prompting. Try carrying around flashcards and glance at one or two from time to time or ask a friend who's also studying for the test to quiz you.

To enhance your retention, look for ways to put the information into practice so that you can apply it rather than simply recalling it. If you're using the information in practical ways, it will be much easier to remember. Similarly, it helps to solidify a concept in your mind if you're not only reading it to yourself but also explaining it to someone else. Ask a friend to let you teach them about a concept you're a little shaky on (or speak aloud to an imaginary audience if necessary). As you try to summarize, define, give examples, and answer your friend's questions, you'll understand the concepts better and they will stay with you longer. Finally, step back for a big picture view and ask yourself how each piece of information fits with the whole subject. When you link the different concepts together and see them working together as a whole, it's easier to remember the individual components.

Finally, practice showing your work on any multi-step problems, even if you're just studying. Writing out each step you take to solve a problem will help solidify the process in your mind, and you'll be more likely to remember it during the test.

Modality

Modality simply refers to the means or method by which you study. Choosing a study modality that fits your own individual learning style is crucial. No two people learn best in exactly the same way, so it's important to know your strengths and use them to your advantage.

For example, if you learn best by visualization, focus on visualizing a concept in your mind and draw an image or a diagram. Try color-coding your notes, illustrating them, or creating symbols that will trigger your mind to recall a learned concept. If you learn best by hearing or discussing information, find a study partner who learns the same way or read aloud to yourself. Think about how to put the information in your own words. Imagine that you are giving a lecture on the topic and record yourself so you can listen to it later.

For any learning style, flashcards can be helpful. Organize the information so you can take advantage of spare moments to review. Underline key words or phrases. Use different colors for different categories. Mnemonic devices (such as creating a short list in which every item starts with the same letter) can also help with retention. Find what works best for you and use it to store the information in your mind most effectively and easily.

Secret Key #3 – Practice the Right Way

Your success on test day depends not only on how many hours you put into preparing, but also on whether you prepared the right way. It's good to check along the way to see if your studying is paying off. One of the most effective ways to do this is by taking practice tests to evaluate your progress. Practice tests are useful because they show exactly where you need to improve. Every time you take a practice test, pay special attention to these three groups of questions:

- The questions you got wrong
- The questions you had to guess on, even if you guessed right
- The questions you found difficult or slow to work through

This will show you exactly what your weak areas are, and where you need to devote more study time. Ask yourself why each of these questions gave you trouble. Was it because you didn't understand the material? Was it because you didn't remember the vocabulary? Do you need more repetitions on this type of question to build speed and confidence? Dig into those questions and figure out how you can strengthen your weak areas as you go back to review the material.

Additionally, many practice tests have a section explaining the answer choices. It can be tempting to read the explanation and think that you now have a good understanding of the concept. However, an explanation likely only covers part of the question's broader context. Even if the explanation makes perfect sense, **go back and investigate** every concept related to the question until you're positive you have a thorough understanding.

As you go along, keep in mind that the practice test is just that: practice. Memorizing these questions and answers will not be very helpful on the actual test because it is unlikely to have any of the same exact questions. If you only know the right answers to the sample questions, you won't be prepared for the real thing. **Study the concepts** until you understand them fully, and then you'll be able to answer any question that shows up on the test.

It's important to wait on the practice tests until you're ready. If you take a test on your first day of study, you may be overwhelmed by the amount of material covered and how much you need to learn. Work up to it gradually.

On test day, you'll need to be prepared for answering questions, managing your time, and using the test-taking strategies you've learned. It's a lot to balance, like a mental marathon that will have a big impact on your future. Like training for a marathon, you'll need to start slowly and work your way up. When test day arrives, you'll be ready.

Start with the strategies you've read in the first two Secret Keys—plan your course and study in the way that works best for you. If you have time, consider using multiple study resources to get different approaches to the same concepts. It can be helpful to see difficult concepts from more than one angle. Then find a good source for practice tests. Many times, the test website will suggest potential study resources or provide sample tests.

Practice Test Strategy

If you're able to find at least three practice tests, we recommend this strategy:

Untimed and Open-Book Practice

Take the first test with no time constraints and with your notes and study guide handy. Take your time and focus on applying the strategies you've learned.

Timed and Open-Book Practice

Take the second practice test open-book as well, but set a timer and practice pacing yourself to finish in time.

Timed and Closed-Book Practice

Take any other practice tests as if it were test day. Set a timer and put away your study materials. Sit at a table or desk in a quiet room, imagine yourself at the testing center, and answer questions as quickly and accurately as possible.

Keep repeating timed and closed-book tests on a regular basis until you run out of practice tests or it's time for the actual test. Your mind will be ready for the schedule and stress of test day, and you'll be able to focus on recalling the material you've learned.

Secret Key #4 – Pace Yourself

Once you're fully prepared for the material on the test, your biggest challenge on test day will be managing your time. Just knowing that the clock is ticking can make you panic even if you have plenty of time left. Work on pacing yourself so you can build confidence against the time constraints of the exam. Pacing is a difficult skill to master, especially in a high-pressure environment, so **practice is vital**.

Set time expectations for your pace based on how much time is available. For example, if a section has 60 questions and the time limit is 30 minutes, you know you have to average 30 seconds or less per question in order to answer them all. Although 30 seconds is the hard limit, set 25 seconds per question as your goal, so you reserve extra time to spend on harder questions. When you budget extra time for the harder questions, you no longer have any reason to stress when those questions take longer to answer.

Don't let this time expectation distract you from working through the test at a calm, steady pace, but keep it in mind so you don't spend too much time on any one question. Recognize that taking extra time on one question you don't understand may keep you from answering two that you do understand later in the test. If your time limit for a question is up and you're still not sure of the answer, mark it and move on, and come back to it later if the time and the test format allow. If the testing format doesn't allow you to return to earlier questions, just make an educated guess; then put it out of your mind and move on.

On the easier questions, be careful not to rush. It may seem wise to hurry through them so you have more time for the challenging ones, but it's not worth missing one if you know the concept and just didn't take the time to read the question fully. Work efficiently but make sure you understand the question and have looked at all of the answer choices, since more than one may seem right at first.

Even if you're paying attention to the time, you may find yourself a little behind at some point. You should speed up to get back on track, but do so wisely. Don't panic; just take a few seconds less on each question until you're caught up. Don't guess without thinking, but do look through the answer choices and eliminate any you know are wrong. If you can get down to two choices, it is often worthwhile to guess from those. Once you've chosen an answer, move on and don't dwell on any that you skipped or had to hurry through. If a question was taking too long, chances are it was one of the harder ones, so you weren't as likely to get it right anyway.

On the other hand, if you find yourself getting ahead of schedule, it may be beneficial to slow down a little. The more quickly you work, the more likely you are to make a careless mistake that will affect your score. You've budgeted time for each question, so don't be afraid to spend that time. Practice an efficient but careful pace to get the most out of the time you have.

Secret Key #5 – Have a Plan for Guessing

When you're taking the test, you may find yourself stuck on a question. Some of the answer choices seem better than others, but you don't see the one answer choice that is obviously correct. What do you do?

The scenario described above is very common, yet most test takers have not effectively prepared for it. Developing and practicing a plan for guessing may be one of the single most effective uses of your time as you get ready for the exam.

In developing your plan for guessing, there are three questions to address:

- When should you start the guessing process?
- How should you narrow down the choices?
- Which answer should you choose?

When to Start the Guessing Process

Unless your plan for guessing is to select C every time (which, despite its merits, is not what we recommend), you need to leave yourself enough time to apply your answer elimination strategies. Since you have a limited amount of time for each question, that means that if you're going to give yourself the best shot at guessing correctly, you have to decide quickly whether or not you will guess.

Of course, the best-case scenario is that you don't have to guess at all, so first, see if you can answer the question based on your knowledge of the subject and basic reasoning skills. Focus on the key words in the question and try to jog your memory of related topics. Give yourself a chance to bring the knowledge to mind, but once you realize that you don't have (or you can't access) the knowledge you need to answer the question, it's time to start the guessing process.

It's almost always better to start the guessing process too early than too late. It only takes a few seconds to remember something and answer the question from knowledge. Carefully eliminating wrong answer choices takes longer. Plus, going through the process of eliminating answer choices can actually help jog your memory.

Summary: Start the guessing process as soon as you decide that you can't answer the question based on your knowledge.

How to Narrow Down the Choices

The next chapter in this book (**Test-Taking Strategies**) includes a wide range of strategies for how to approach questions and how to look for answer choices to eliminate. You will definitely want to read those carefully, practice them, and figure out which ones work best for you. Here though, we're going to address a mindset rather than a particular strategy.

Your odds of guessing an answer correctly depend on how many options you are choosing from.

Number of options left	5	4	3	2	1
Odds of guessing correctly	20%	25%	33%	50%	100%

You can see from this chart just how valuable it is to be able to eliminate incorrect answers and make an educated guess, but there are two things that many test takers do that cause them to miss out on the benefits of guessing:

- Accidentally eliminating the correct answer
- Selecting an answer based on an impression

We'll look at the first one here, and the second one in the next section.

To avoid accidentally eliminating the correct answer, we recommend a thought exercise called **the $5 challenge**. In this challenge, you only eliminate an answer choice from contention if you are willing to bet $5 on it being wrong. Why $5? Five dollars is a small but not insignificant amount of money. It's an amount you could afford to lose but wouldn't want to throw away. And while losing $5 once might not hurt too much, doing it twenty times will set you back $100. In the same way, each small decision you make—eliminating a choice here, guessing on a question there—won't by itself impact your score very much, but when you put them all together, they can make a big difference. By holding each answer choice elimination decision to a higher standard, you can reduce the risk of accidentally eliminating the correct answer.

The $5 challenge can also be applied in a positive sense: If you are willing to bet $5 that an answer choice *is* correct, go ahead and mark it as correct.

Summary: Only eliminate an answer choice if you are willing to bet $5 that it is wrong.

Which Answer to Choose

You're taking the test. You've run into a hard question and decided you'll have to guess. You've eliminated all the answer choices you're willing to bet $5 on. Now you have to pick an answer. Why do we even need to talk about this? Why can't you just pick whichever one you feel like when the time comes?

The answer to these questions is that if you don't come into the test with a plan, you'll rely on your impression to select an answer choice, and if you do that, you risk falling into a trap. The test writers know that everyone who takes their test will be guessing on some of the questions, so they intentionally write wrong answer choices to seem plausible. You still have to pick an answer though, and if the wrong answer choices are designed to look right, how can you ever be sure that you're not falling for their trap? The best solution we've found to this dilemma is to take the decision out of your hands entirely. Here is the process we recommend:

Once you've eliminated any choices that you are confident (willing to bet $5) are wrong, select the first remaining choice as your answer.

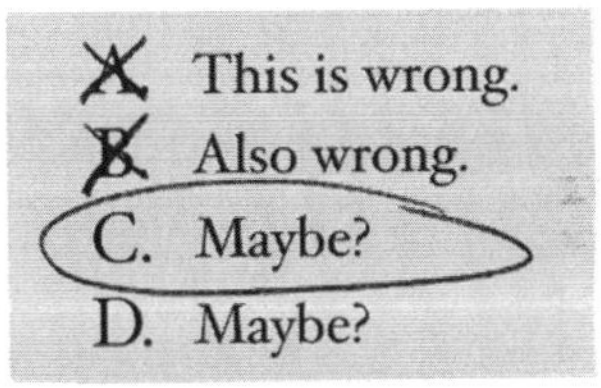

Whether you choose to select the first remaining choice, the second, or the last, the important thing is that you use some preselected standard. Using this approach guarantees that you will not be enticed into selecting an answer choice that looks right, because you are not basing your decision on how the answer choices look.

This is not meant to make you question your knowledge. Instead, it is to help you recognize the difference between your knowledge and your impressions. There's a huge difference between thinking an answer is right because of what you know, and thinking an answer is right because it looks or sounds like it should be right.

Summary: To ensure that your selection is appropriately random, make a predetermined selection from among all answer choices you have not eliminated.

Test-Taking Strategies

This section contains a list of test-taking strategies that you may find helpful as you work through the test. By taking what you know and applying logical thought, you can maximize your chances of answering any question correctly!

It is very important to realize that every question is different and every person is different: no single strategy will work on every question, and no single strategy will work for every person. That's why we've included all of them here, so you can try them out and determine which ones work best for different types of questions and which ones work best for you.

Question Strategies

✓ Read Carefully

Read the question and the answer choices carefully. Don't miss the question because you misread the terms. You have plenty of time to read each question thoroughly and make sure you understand what is being asked. Yet a happy medium must be attained, so don't waste too much time. You must read carefully and efficiently.

✓ Contextual Clues

Look for contextual clues. If the question includes a word you are not familiar with, look at the immediate context for some indication of what the word might mean. Contextual clues can often give you all the information you need to decipher the meaning of an unfamiliar word. Even if you can't determine the meaning, you may be able to narrow down the possibilities enough to make a solid guess at the answer to the question.

✓ Prefixes

If you're having trouble with a word in the question or answer choices, try dissecting it. Take advantage of every clue that the word might include. Prefixes can be a huge help. Usually, they allow you to determine a basic meaning. *Pre-* means before, *post-* means after, *pro-* is positive, *de-* is negative. From prefixes, you can get an idea of the general meaning of the word and try to put it into context.

✓ Hedge Words

Watch out for critical hedge words, such as *likely, may, can, often, almost, mostly, usually, generally, rarely*, and *sometimes*. Question writers insert these hedge phrases to cover every possibility. Often an answer choice will be wrong simply because it leaves no room for exception. Be on guard for answer choices that have definitive words such as *exactly* and *always*.

✓ Switchback Words

Stay alert for *switchbacks*. These are the words and phrases frequently used to alert you to shifts in thought. The most common switchback words are *but, although*, and *however*. Others include *nevertheless, on the other hand, even though, while, in spite of, despite*, and *regardless of*. Switchback words are important to catch because they can change the direction of the question or an answer choice.

⊘ Face Value

When in doubt, use common sense. Accept the situation in the problem at face value. Don't read too much into it. These problems will not require you to make wild assumptions. If you have to go beyond creativity and warp time or space in order to have an answer choice fit the question, then you should move on and consider the other answer choices. These are normal problems rooted in reality. The applicable relationship or explanation may not be readily apparent, but it is there for you to figure out. Use your common sense to interpret anything that isn't clear.

Answer Choice Strategies

⊘ Answer Selection

The most thorough way to pick an answer choice is to identify and eliminate wrong answers until only one is left, then confirm it is the correct answer. Sometimes an answer choice may immediately seem right, but be careful. The test writers will usually put more than one reasonable answer choice on each question, so take a second to read all of them and make sure that the other choices are not equally obvious. As long as you have time left, it is better to read every answer choice than to pick the first one that looks right without checking the others.

⊘ Answer Choice Families

An answer choice family consists of two (in rare cases, three) answer choices that are very similar in construction and cannot all be true at the same time. If you see two answer choices that are direct opposites or parallels, one of them is usually the correct answer. For instance, if one answer choice says that quantity *x* increases and another either says that quantity *x* decreases (opposite) or says that quantity *y* increases (parallel), then those answer choices would fall into the same family. An answer choice that doesn't match the construction of the answer choice family is more likely to be incorrect. Most questions will not have answer choice families, but when they do appear, you should be prepared to recognize them.

⊘ Eliminate Answers

Eliminate answer choices as soon as you realize they are wrong, but make sure you consider all possibilities. If you are eliminating answer choices and realize that the last one you are left with is also wrong, don't panic. Start over and consider each choice again. There may be something you missed the first time that you will realize on the second pass.

⊘ Avoid Fact Traps

Don't be distracted by an answer choice that is factually true but doesn't answer the question. You are looking for the choice that answers the question. Stay focused on what the question is asking for so you don't accidentally pick an answer that is true but incorrect. Always go back to the question and make sure the answer choice you've selected actually answers the question and is not merely a true statement.

⊘ Extreme Statements

In general, you should avoid answers that put forth extreme actions as standard practice or proclaim controversial ideas as established fact. An answer choice that states the "process should be used in certain situations, if..." is much more likely to be correct than one that states the "process should be discontinued completely." The first is a calm rational statement and doesn't even make a definitive, uncompromising stance, using a hedge word *if* to provide wiggle room, whereas the second choice is far more extreme.

☑ Benchmark

As you read through the answer choices and you come across one that seems to answer the question well, mentally select that answer choice. This is not your final answer, but it's the one that will help you evaluate the other answer choices. The one that you selected is your benchmark or standard for judging each of the other answer choices. Every other answer choice must be compared to your benchmark. That choice is correct until proven otherwise by another answer choice beating it. If you find a better answer, then that one becomes your new benchmark. Once you've decided that no other choice answers the question as well as your benchmark, you have your final answer.

☑ Predict the Answer

Before you even start looking at the answer choices, it is often best to try to predict the answer. When you come up with the answer on your own, it is easier to avoid distractions and traps because you will know exactly what to look for. The right answer choice is unlikely to be word-for-word what you came up with, but it should be a close match. Even if you are confident that you have the right answer, you should still take the time to read each option before moving on.

General Strategies

☑ Tough Questions

If you are stumped on a problem or it appears too hard or too difficult, don't waste time. Move on! Remember though, if you can quickly check for obviously incorrect answer choices, your chances of guessing correctly are greatly improved. Before you completely give up, at least try to knock out a couple of possible answers. Eliminate what you can and then guess at the remaining answer choices before moving on.

☑ Check Your Work

Since you will probably not know every term listed and the answer to every question, it is important that you get credit for the ones that you do know. Don't miss any questions through careless mistakes. If at all possible, try to take a second to look back over your answer selection and make sure you've selected the correct answer choice and haven't made a costly careless mistake (such as marking an answer choice that you didn't mean to mark). This quick double check should more than pay for itself in caught mistakes for the time it costs.

☑ Pace Yourself

It's easy to be overwhelmed when you're looking at a page full of questions; your mind is confused and full of random thoughts, and the clock is ticking down faster than you would like. Calm down and maintain the pace that you have set for yourself. Especially as you get down to the last few minutes of the test, don't let the small numbers on the clock make you panic. As long as you are on track by monitoring your pace, you are guaranteed to have time for each question.

☑ Don't Rush

It is very easy to make errors when you are in a hurry. Maintaining a fast pace in answering questions is pointless if it makes you miss questions that you would have gotten right otherwise. Test writers like to include distracting information and wrong answers that seem right. Taking a little extra time to avoid careless mistakes can make all the difference in your test score. Find a pace that allows you to be confident in the answers that you select.

✓ Keep Moving

Panicking will not help you pass the test, so do your best to stay calm and keep moving. Taking deep breaths and going through the answer elimination steps you practiced can help to break through a stress barrier and keep your pace.

Final Notes

The combination of a solid foundation of content knowledge and the confidence that comes from practicing your plan for applying that knowledge is the key to maximizing your performance on test day. As your foundation of content knowledge is built up and strengthened, you'll find that the strategies included in this chapter become more and more effective in helping you quickly sift through the distractions and traps of the test to isolate the correct answer.

Now that you're preparing to move forward into the test content chapters of this book, be sure to keep your goal in mind. As you read, think about how you will be able to apply this information on the test. If you've already seen sample questions for the test and you have an idea of the question format and style, try to come up with questions of your own that you can answer based on what you're reading. This will give you valuable practice applying your knowledge in the same ways you can expect to on test day.

Good luck and good studying!

Music Theory and Analysis

Theory and Composition

Scale Degrees

A scale degree is an assigned number to the sequential notes of any major or minor scale. Since the Western tonal language is transposable in all keys, this systematic approach to music theory aids comprehensive musical analysis. The pitches of any major or minor scale are numbered 1–7, indicated with upper-case Roman numerals for major harmonies and lower-case Roman numerals for minor harmonies. When not modified by accidentals, a major key signature renders these harmonies by pitch: I, ii, iii, IV, V, vi, and vii^{o} (diminished). Each scale degree is also given a name:

- I - tonic
- II - supertonic
- III - mediant
- IV - subdominant
- V - dominant
- VI - submediant
- VII - leading tone or subtonic

The **scale degrees** in Western tonal music function similarly in any diatonic scale, and conventions can be generalized, such as the stable importance of the tonic or the tendency for the leading tone to progress to the tonic.

Inversions of Triads and Seventh Chords

Chords are related by inversion if they contain the same pitches with the same root, but have different pitches sounding in the bass. For **triads**, a chord is considered to be in root position if the root of the chord is the lowest-sounding pitch. A triad is considered to be in **first inversion** if the third of the chord is the lowest-sounding pitch. A triad is considered to be in **second inversion** if the fifth of the chord is the lowest-sounding pitch. For example, the root position triad g-b-d becomes b-d-g' in first inversion and d-g'-b' in second inversion. For seventh chords, the classifications are similar except for the addition of a **third inversion**, indicating that the seventh of the chord is the lowest-sounding pitch. Thus, for the root position seventh chord g-b-d-f, first inversion is b-d-f-g', second inversion is d-f-g'-b', and third inversion is f-g'-b'-d'.

Harmonic Analysis Nomenclature

Recall that the pitches of any major or minor scale are numbered 1–7, indicated with upper-case Roman numerals for major harmonies and lower-case Roman numerals for minor harmonies. There is also conventional nomenclature to cover the many variations of these harmonies. A diminished triad is indicated by a superscript o (e.g., vii^{o}). A first inversion triad, which has the third of the chord rather than the root as its bass, is indicated by a superscript 6 (e.g., I^{6}). A second inversion harmony, which has the fifth of the chord rather than the root as its bass, is indicated by a superscript 6/4 (e.g., IV$^{6/4}$).

Harmonies with an added seventh (root, third, fifth, and seventh) use a similar notation. A seventh chord in root position is indicated by a superscript 7 (e.g., V^{7}). A seventh chord in first inversion uses the superscript 6/5 (e.g., V$^{6/5}$), in second inversion uses the superscript 4/3 (e.g., V$^{4/3}$), and in third inversion uses the superscript 4/2 (e.g., V$^{4/2}$).

Authentic Cadence

The authentic cadence is defined as a dominant-sounding harmony resolving to the tonic harmony, notated as V-I or V-i in Western tonal theory. The **authentic cadence** is considered to be the strongest cadence because of the presence of the supertonic to tonic progression as well as the leading tone-to-tonic progression. In voice leading, these two progressions exhibit the highest tension and release movements within music theory. An authentic cadence can be either perfect or imperfect. A **perfect authentic cadence** has both the roots of the V and I chords sounding in the bass, and the tonic as the highest-sounding note on the final chord. An **imperfect authentic cadence** does not involve all the conditions required to be a perfect authentic cadence, and so it may not have the tonic sounding in the highest note of the final chord, or it may have inverted chords.

Plagal Cadence

The plagal cadence is defined as the subdominant sounding harmony resolving to the tonic harmony, notated as IV-I or iv-i in Western tonal theory. Since there is the absence of a leading tone resolution in a **plagal cadence**, it is not considered as final or as strong of a cadence as the authentic cadence. Oftentimes, the plagal cadence is found as an extension of an authentic cadence, embellishing the final tonic through the neighboring notes of the third and fourth scale degrees, and of the fifth and sixth scale degrees. The plagal cadence is a common ending to many Protestant hymns, and is also known as the **amen cadence**, as the cadence is set to the word amen. The plagal cadence is so closely associated with Protestant hymns that some composers have used the IV-I progression as an allusion to its sacred usage.

Half Cadence

The half cadence is defined as any harmony progressing to a dominant harmony. The preceding harmony can be the tonic, subdominant, supertonic, or any other harmony. A common **half cadence** is the tonic in second inversion resolving to the dominant, notated as $I^{6/4}$-V in Western tonal theory. This particular half cadence is known as the cadential tonic six-four, and shares the bass note from the six-four chord with the resulting dominant chord. Oftentimes, the cadential tonic six-four progression occurs at the end of the first section in a two-part or binary piece of music. Other types of half cadences include the **Phrygian half cadence**, in which a first inversion subdominant chord proceeds to the dominant similarly in the Phrygian mode, and the Lydian half cadence, in which a first inversion subdominant chord is raised by a half step and then resolved to the dominant.

Deceptive Cadence

The deceptive cadence is defined as the dominant-sounding harmony progressing to a harmony that defies the expected tonic harmony, most commonly the submediant harmony. The leading tone of the dominant resolves to the tonic of the key, but the tonic pitch acts as either the third or fifth of the chord, instead of the root. The dominant chord in deceptive cadences can progress to the submediant harmony, notated as V-VI or V-vi, or to the subdominant harmony, notated as V-IV or V-iv. The **deceptive cadence** is an important compositional tool in avoiding an ending, and is useful not only in delaying or prolonging an ending, but also in transitioning to another structural section of music. This cadence is considered to be a **weak cadence**, as there is little to no sense of resolution in the music. Another name for the deceptive cadence is the interrupted cadence.

Circle of Fifths

The circle of fifths describes the relationship and pattern of major and minor keys from one to the next as they move up or down in fifths. Moving up a fifth from C becomes G; moving up a fifth from

G becomes D; and moving up a fifth from D becomes A, etc. The **circle of fifths** is modeled so that eventually, with enharmonic naming, it goes through all 12 keys back to C. As each key moves along the circle, a sharp or flat is added depending on the direction of the circle. For example, the key of C major has zero flats; moving down a fifth, F major has one flat; moving down another fifth, Bb has two flats, etc. The circle of fifths can be applied to both major keys and to minor keys, and is also useful in determining the degree of relatedness among keys.

Natural, Melodic, and Harmonic Minors

In Western tonal theory, the minor scale is the following pattern of whole and half steps: whole-half-whole-whole-half-whole-whole. The **minor scale** is similar to the Aeolian mode of the Renaissance era. This minor scale without alterations is termed the **natural minor scale**, or the pure minor scale. If the minor scale is altered so that the seventh note of the scale is raised by a half step, then it is termed the **harmonic minor scale**. If the minor scale is altered so that both the sixth and the seventh notes of the scale are raised by a half step in ascending motion, and lowered to the natural minor in descending motion, then the scale is termed **melodic minor scale**. These patterns can be applied to any of the 12 pitches to produce the natural, melodic, and harmonic minor scales.

Whole Tone Scale and the Chromatic Scale

The whole tone scale is a scale in which every pitch is separated by a whole step. Within Western musical tonality, there are two different whole tone scales, each made up of six pitches. The **whole tone scale** can be either C-D-E-F#-G#-A# or C#-D#-F-G-A-B. The **chromatic scale**, on the other hand, is a scale in which every pitch is separated by a half step. Within Western musical tonality, the chromatic scale includes all 12 pitches of an octave. Both the whole tone scale and the chromatic scale lack a clear tonal center, as either of the scales could start on any key without any definite hierarchy to the pattern. However, composers tend to use the chromatic scale as a tool to increase complexity, while the whole tone scale is a useful tool to give a feeling of vague spaciousness.

12-Tone Music

Twelve-tone music is a system of musical theory in which a composition is based on a serial ordering of all 12 pitches that stipulates the sequence in which those 12 pitches should appear in the composition. The **12-tone system of music** arose as a result of the growing disdain for traditional tonal music. This theory of composition became a way for music to be planned in an abstract manner, into a serial row that establishes the pitch structure of the resulting composition. Rows can be manipulated throughout the composition through retrograde, inversion, or retrograde-inversion. The rows can also be transposed to start on a different pitch wherein the same intervallic relationship of the row is kept intact. Arnold Schoenberg, a leading Austrian composer of the Second Viennese School, began to develop this theory of composition in the early 1920s and continued to compose 12-tone music throughout the 20th century.

Tonal vs. Real Answer to a Fugal Subject

The **fugue** is a form of imitative counterpoint in which a fugue theme is introduced at the beginning of the work, also known as the exposition, and is echoed in all of the fugal voices though imitation and development. The term *fugue* comes from the Latin *fugere* meaning "to flee," as each voice essentially chases the previous voice. The initial subject is called the leader, or **dux**, and is presented in the tonic key. The dux is usually followed by the **comes**, the companion answer in the dominant key, which can be presented in one of two ways: real or tonal. In a **real answer** to a fugal subject, the theme is transposed exactly note to note in the dominant key. In a **tonal answer** to a fugal subject, the theme is transposed loosely in the dominant key, modified so as to maintain harmonic congruity or to facilitate modulations.

Tone Cluster

A tone cluster is a group of closely spaced notes played simultaneously, usually in intervals of adjacent seconds and groupings, or "clusters." The term usually refers to stacks of more than two neighboring notes, with three being the minimum. **Tone clusters** can be diatonic, chromatic, and dia-chromatic. For **diatonic tone clusters**, only neighboring notes in the diatonic key are used. For **chromatic tone clusters**, notes that are separated by a half-step are used. For **dia-chromatic tone clusters**, both diatonic seconds and chromatic notes are used. Tone clusters were not considered a definite compositional tool until the 1900s, and they appeared rarely before that time. The concept of "tone cluster" was termed by the American composer Henry Cowell (1897–1965) in the 1920s, and appears in compositions by Western classical composers such as Charles Ives, Béla Bartók, Lou Harrison, Olivier Messiaen, Karlheinz Stockhausen, and George Crumb, as well as in jazz and popular music.

Italian Tempo Markings

The tempo marking **adagio** comes from the Italian ad agio meaning, "at ease," and is understood to mean a slower tempo than andante, but faster than largo. The tempo marking **moderato** means "moderately" in Italian, and is a relative tempo designation that is faster than andante, but slower than allegro. The tempo marking **presto** means "very fast" in Italian, and is generally treated as a very quick tempo, much faster than allegro. The marking of **prestissimo** indicates a tempo as fast as possible. The tempo marking **andante** means "at a walking pace" in Italian, and is a more ambiguous tempo that can be thought of as faster than adagio but slower than allegro. The tempo marking **allegro** means "lively, merry" in Italian, and is generally treated as a fast or moderately fast tempo.

Hemiola

The term *hemiola* comes from the Greek meaning "one and a half," also known as the ratio of three to two. Its use in ancient Greek and Latin musical theory referred to the interval of the fifth, as the fifth is made up of two strings with lengths of 3:2. **Hemiola** also refers to the rhythm of three notes in a space that usually only has two notes, whether in succession or simultaneously. **Horizontal hemiola**, or a hemiola in succession, refers to a change in note values where, for example, three half notes follow a measure of two dotted half notes in 6/4 meter. **Vertical hemiola**, or a hemiola that occurs simultaneously, refers to a rhythmic syncopation where, for example, three quarter notes play over two dotted quarter notes in 6/8 meter. However, music theorists prefer to use the Latin term **sesquialtera** in cases of vertical hemiola as a more accurate representation of the three-against-two rhythm.

Metrical Accenting

Metrical accenting refers to the natural stresses on certain beats of a meter. This can be defined by the meter itself or by the style or origin of the musical rhythm. In a simple 3/4 meter, the tendency for a metrical accent falls on the first beat of the measure. However, in certain musical styles, such as the Polish mazurka and other folk dances, the metrical stress may be on the second beat in 3/4 meter. In 4/4 meter, there is naturally a primary stress on the downbeat of the measure, and a secondary, weaker stress on the third beat of the measure. However, in certain jazz and world music, the accents may be on the second and fourth beats for stylistic accuracy. In compound meters such as 6/8, 9/8, and 12/8 time, there is a natural accent on the first of every group of three eighth notes.

Compound vs. Simple Meters

In both simple and compound meters, the numbers in the meter refer to the subdivision of beats within a musical measure. The number on the top, also known as the numerator, specifies the number of pulses or beats in a measure. The number on the bottom, also known as the denominator, specifies which note-value gets a pulse. For example, in 2/4 meter, there are two beats per measure, with the quarter note receiving each pulse. **Simple meters** cannot be subdivided into smaller groups, and they include meters such as 2/4, 4/4, 2/2, 4/2, 5/4, and 3/4. In a **compound meter**, the number of pulses can be subdivided into groups of three. For example, 6/8 meter has two beats which can be subdivided into six pulses per measure. Here, the dotted quarter note receives the beat, while the eighth note receives the pulse. Other examples of compound meters include 9/8 and 12/8 meters.

Simple and Compound Musical Form

Simple musical form describes a tonal work that can be seen as a complete and self-contained work that is not divisible into other, smaller self-contained works. Examples of **simple musical forms** include binary and ternary forms. In each of these forms, there are thematic sections labeled A or B, but neither of these thematic sections can be further divisible into other simple forms. **Compound musical form** describes a tonal work that can be seen as a composite form that is made up of other, smaller simple forms such as binary and ternary forms. An example of a compound form is the Minuetto and Trio, in which the simple Minuetto form surrounds the simple binary Trio form to create an overall ternary compound form. Other examples of compound musical forms are sonata movements, symphony movements, string quartets, and suites.

Binary vs. Rounded Binary Form

Form refers to the structure of a musical composition with regard to thematic, tonal, dynamic, and textural structure. **Binary form** consists of two main sections, both repeated. The first section, labeled A, presents the home key (sometimes referred to as "tonic key") of the composition. The second section, A', is often labeled B but is more precisely a modified version of A; the musical material of A' is often in the dominant key if the tonic was major, or in the relative major key if the tonic was minor. Simple binary form is considered to be an open form, as neither A nor A' can exist independently. In a **rounded binary form**, there is a return to the original thematic material of A. Thus, the form can be represented as ABA or AA'A. The initial A section as well as the A' (or B) section are both repeated as in simple binary form and should not be confused with ternary form.

Ternary Form

Ternary form consists of three main sections in which the first and third sections are nearly identical with a contrasting second section. The first section, labeled A, presents the home key (sometimes referred to as "tonic key") of the composition, and returns at the end of the composition in the third section, also labeled A. The middle section, labeled B, is usually in a related key and cadences in the same key or another closely related key before the third section begins. In ternary form, sections may repeat, but it is not required, and the middle section is usually distinctly different, labeled B instead of A'. Ternary form is considered to be a closed form, since all three sections could exist independently.

Monophony, Homophony, Polyphony, and Heterophony

The term **monophony** refers to the texture of any music that is made up of a single melodic line. The melodic line can be performed by a solo musician or by a group of musicians. Examples include plainchant, minnesinger, Meistersinger, and troubadour music. The term **homophony** refers to the texture of any music that is made up of a main melodic line over a supporting accompaniment.

Examples include most rock, pop, country, and jazz music. The term **polyphony** refers to the texture of any music that is made up of many equally important melodic lines. Examples include much of Renaissance and Baroque music. The term **heterophony** refers to the texture of any music that is made up of multiple improvised interpretations of the same melody played at the same time. Heterophony mostly occurs in non-Western music cultures such as those of East Asia, South Asia, Southeast Asia, and the Middle East.

Equal- and Unequal-Voice Polyphony

The term **polyphony** refers to the texture of any music that is made up of many equally important melodic lines. Examples include much of Renaissance and Baroque music. Within polyphony are equal- and unequal-voice polyphony. **Equal-voice polyphony** refers to polyphony that maintains the same thematic material in all the individual voices. A prime example of equal-voice polyphony is the canon, in which the exact same melodic material enters sequentially after a uniform time interval. Other examples of equal-voice polyphony include fugues, inventions, and other forms of imitation. **Unequal-voice polyphony** refers to polyphony in which greater importance is given to one or more melodic lines. Examples of unequal-voice polyphony include Medieval-era cantus firmus compositions that give musical precedence to the main tune, usually sung or played in the tenor voice.

Basic Music Theory Concepts when Composing

Teaching Musical Units Leading to Basic Composition

When teaching basic composition, the curriculum should entail several introductory concepts that sequentially lead to the understanding and creation of musical patterns. The beginning lessons should cover elements of **notation** as well as the understanding and appreciation of musical patterns. The students should learn treble clef, meter, bar line, measure, staff, octave, and intervals. Students should also examine a theme and variation, to learn how musical patterns can function. Students should start with short eight-measure phrases, working on the sequencing and patterning of music. The instructor should use highly imaginative examples to demonstrate **sound patterning**, such as a percussive interpretation of a thunderstorm or the sound a hopping frog might make. As the students learn to integrate their imagination with musical sounds, the lesson sequencing can focus more on musical compositional techniques such as transcriptions, cadences, and different tonalities.

Contrary Motion, Parallel Motion, Similar Motion, and Oblique Motion

Contrary motion, parallel motion, similar motion, and oblique motion all refer to the simultaneous movement of two or more musical lines. The terms can describe both vocal and instrumental musical lines moving in parts at the same time. **Contrary motion** refers to the motion of two musical lines that move in opposite directions. **Parallel motion** refers to the motion of two musical lines that move in the same direction, whether upwards or downwards, while maintaining the same interval between the lines. **Similar motion** refers to the motion of two musical lines that move in similar directions, whether upwards or downwards, but without maintaining the same interval between the lines. **Oblique motion** refers to the motion of two musical lines in which one line stays stationary while the other musical line moves in an upward or downward direction.

Types of Dissonance Found in Tonal Counterpoint

In tonal counterpoint, careful regulations have been made to avoid dissonances; however, certain types of dissonances are allowed in the form of voice-leading treatments. If an anticipation tone is dissonant yet unaccented, it is allowed if it is then directly reharmonized. Dissonance is also allowed in the cambiata, a figure that usually moves down a second to a dissonant pitch, down another third to a consonant pitch, then up a second that can be dissonant or consonant. Another form of allowable dissonance is the **appoggiatura**, in which there is a leap to a dissonance followed by a descending step. Also allowed is a **suspension**, in which a dissonance tone sounds on a downbeat and is then resolved downward by step. A **passing tone** moves in a stepwise motion through two consonant tones. A **neighbor tone** also moves in a stepwise motion but returns to the original consonant tone. An **escape tone** is a dissonant note that is approached by step and resolved by a leap in the opposite direction.

Interval Types

Intervals measure the semitones, or half-steps, between any two tones in Western music theory; additional information can be applied through five descriptive adjectives: perfect, major, minor, diminished, and augmented. A **perfect interval** only refers to the unison, fourth, fifth, and octave; when any perfect interval is lowered by a half-step, it becomes a **diminished interval**. When any perfect interval is raised by a half-step, it becomes an **augmented interval**. Major intervals can refer to the second, third, sixth, and seventh intervals. **Major intervals** occur in a diatonic major scale and measure the relationships between those two pitches. When any major interval is lowered by a half-step, it becomes a **minor interval**. When any minor interval is lowered by a half-step, it becomes a **diminished interval**. When any major interval is raised by a half-step, it becomes an augmented interval.

Relative Minor vs. Parallel Minor

For any diatonic major scale, there exists a relative minor and parallel minor of that scale. The **relative minor scale** shares the same key signature as the major scale. The **parallel minor scale** shares only the same tonic pitch. F major, for example, has the relative minor scale of d minor (which shares the same key signature of one flat) and the parallel minor scale of f minor (which shares the same tonic pitch of F). Both the relative minor and the parallel minor scales are frequently used as common keys to modulate to within a composition. In the relative minor, composers can easily modulate to a relative minor by using any of the shared chords, since the key signature is identical for the relative major and minor keys. Parallel minor keys offer the same dominant chord as the parallel major key, but have less in common, since the key signatures of parallel major and minor chords are unrelated.

Clefs Commonly Used in Orchestral Writing

The four main clefs commonly used in orchestral writing are the treble, alto, tenor, and bass clefs. The **treble clef**, also known as the G-clef, is shaped so that the spiral of the symbol circles the G-line on the staff. The instruments that typically employ the treble clef include the violin, woodwinds, high basses, and the treble range of keyboard instruments. The **alto clef**, also known as the C-clef, is shaped so that the middle point of the symbol rests on the third line as middle C. The instrument that typically employs the alto clef is the viola. The **tenor clef** also uses the C-clef, but is placed so that the middle point of the symbol rests on the fourth line as middle C. Instruments that sometimes use the tenor clef include the cello, bassoon, and trombone. The **bass clef**, also known as the F-clef, is shaped so that two dots of the symbol surround the F-line. Instruments that typically employ the bass clef include the double bass, cello, bassoon, trombone, low brasses, and the bass range of keyboard instruments.

Concert Band Instruments vs. Symphonic Band Instruments

Both concert bands and symphonic bands employ a wide range of instruments, and both include the brass family, the woodwind family, and the percussion family, as well as a wide variety of timbres, colors, and ranges. The **concert band** focuses on popular band music and orchestral transcriptions, while the symphonic band is more comparable to a symphonic orchestra in range. The concert band has prescribed parts for two flutes, two oboes, two bassoons, three clarinets, one bass clarinet, four saxophones, four horns, three trumpets, three trombones, one baritone horn, one tuba, and three or four percussion instruments, with a total of 40–50 performers. The **symphonic band** tends to have larger sections with a total of 90–120 performers, and may include the string bass, piccolo, English horn, harp, bass trombone, contrabassoon, and/or a saxophone.

Conventional Parts of Four-Part Harmony

In four-part harmony, the conventional parts from high to low are soprano, alto, tenor, and bass. The general vocal range of the **alto voice** is from F3 to D5. The general vocal range of the **soprano voice** is from C4, middle C, to A5; the general vocal range of the **tenor voice** is from B2 to G4; and the general vocal range of the **bass vocal** range is from E2 to C4. Other vocal parts include the baritone and the mezzo-soprano; the general vocal range of the **baritone** is from G2 to E4, and the general range of the **mezzo-soprano** is from A3 to F5. Although many composers use these ranges in writing a piece of four-part harmony, the voice as an instrument remains one of the most complex of instruments, as each individual's voice can vary drastically in range and ability.

Standard Instrumentation of the Concert Band

The standard instrumentation of the concert band was prescribed by members of the **American Band Association** and helped to cultivate the concert band as an essential performing ensemble in American musical culture. With the standardization of concert band instrumentation in the early 20th century, publishers Boosey & Company and Chappell & Company helped to grow the repertoire of concert bands, especially for the school and community settings. The American Band Association prescribed the **concert band** as having parts for two flutes, two oboes, two bassoons, three clarinets, one bass clarinet, four saxophones, four horns, three trumpets, three trombones, one baritone horn, one tuba, and three or four percussion instruments, with a total of 40–50 performers.

Classical Orchestra Instrument Families

In the Classical era (~1750–1830 AD), music became highly homophonic with a focus on melody and accompaniment textural form. To accommodate for the change in compositional form, the **Classical orchestra** shifted the way it used certain instrument families. In the Baroque era, strings and winds were often doubled to play certain lines. With the advent of melodic authority, first violins were now the dominant string section while the lower strings became the supporting background, both harmonically and rhythmically. Wind parts were simplified from the Baroque contrapuntal lines and were now supporting background harmonies as well. As the Classical era progressed, Mozart (1756–1791) eventually restored the wind section's melodic role within the orchestra. During the Classical era, the bassoon became increasingly independent, as opposed to the previous Baroque setting of the bassoon as part of the bass line. Brass also began to be used in a greater independent capacity during the Classical period.

How Musical Sounds Vary

Classical Singing Timbre vs. Popular Music Timbre

Both classical and popular vocal music traditions strive to create a beautiful sound through singing. However, because of differing aesthetics, the two different traditions hold many different vocal techniques. In **classical singing**, the mouth cavity is trained to have a high palate as in a yawn to create an open, formal sound. In **popular singing**, there is much more flexibility to the shape of the mouth, and many singers use both high and low palates to manipulate the different vocal sounds. Classical singers are encouraged to use a rich, wide **vibrato** to add to the color of the singing tone, while popular singers use less vibrato in their songs. Also, classical singers focus on producing pure vowel tones and clear consonants, while popular singers use a wide variety of sounds, timbres, and techniques such as the rasp, growl, and edge, to achieve emotional range.

Classically Trained Voice

The register of a voice refers to a range of pitches that have a similar tonal quality produced by similar vocal production. In singing, there are three general registers: for men, they are typically the chest, head, and falsetto; for women, they are called the chest, middle, and head voices. The **chest register** refers to the lower ranges of the voice and are said to have a heavier tonal quality similar to that of the natural talking voice. The **head voice**, or the **middle voice** for women, refers to the upper ranges of the voice and is said to have a lighter tonal quality that is not falsetto. **Falsetto**, or the **head voice** for women, refers to the highest ranges of the voice above the normal speaking voice and is said to have a breathy, fairy tonal quality that lacks a lot of overtones.

Physiological Mechanisms of Singing

When using the voice as an instrument, it is important to understand the physiological mechanisms involved in producing sound. The three main vocal parts involved in creating sound are the air supply, vibrator, and resonator. **Air supply** is taken into the lungs by the inspiratory muscles, especially the diaphragm, and emptied from the lungs by the expiratory muscles. The **vibrators** for singing are the vocal folds, held within the voice box or larynx at the top of the trachea. When air passes through the vocal folds through the opening called the glottis, the vocal folds vibrate and produce sound. The sound passes through the **resonators**, principally the pharynx and the mouth cavities. These resonators influence the tonal quality of the sound through the cavity shapes and surfaces, as well as the various singing techniques used to alter sound and timbre.

Relation of Tonal Characteristics to Their Use in Orchestration

The orchestrator uses the tonal characteristics of the different instrument families to meticulously layer each sound into a collective whole. The **strings** tend to have a rich tonal quality and form the basis of many orchestral textures. Strings have a variety of sounds and techniques and can easily function as melody, supporting harmony, or rhythmic texture. **High brasses** have a clear, focused tonal quality and many times are used melodically or as a crisp rhythmic flourish. **Low brasses** tend to provide bass lines as well as rhythmic motives. **Woodwinds** have held various roles within the orchestra and can easily function as melody, supporting harmony, or rhythmic texture, similar to strings. **Percussive instruments** have historically held a rhythmic role in orchestral writing, but have also been used as melodic interest through the marimba, timpani, and other melodic percussion instruments.

How Sound is Produced

Brass Instruments

Brass instruments typically produce sound through the buzzing of the player's lips as the air travels through a tubular, expanding metallic wind instrument. The lips act as a vibrating valve that produces oscillating air and pressure. As the air vibrates through the tubular instrument, some of the energy is lost as viscous and thermal energy, while the rest emerges from the instrument as sound. Almost all **brass instruments** consist of a tube that gets larger toward the end of the tube called the **bell**. The tube is often coiled so that the instrument is easier for the player to hold. Brass instruments resonate at certain frequencies more easily than others, so to produce other tones, players can change the length of the instruments through **valves** or **slides**. Narrower, more cylindrical brass instruments like the trumpet and the trombone produce sharp and clear sounds, while wider, larger-belled brass instruments like the French horn and euphonium produce warmer, darker sounds.

Stringed Instruments

Stringed instruments produce sound through the vibrations of the strings on a resonating body usually made of wood. The **strings**, made of nylon, steel, or silk, can be set in motion by plucking, bowing, or striking. As the string sets the surrounding air in motion, it also vibrates the **soundboard** through the bridge as the resonant vibrator and the audible tone effuses out of the instrument through a sound hole. Pitches on a stringed instrument are modified by string tension, thickness, and length: the higher the tension, the higher the pitch; the thicker the string, the lower the pitch; and the longer the string, the lower the pitch. Strings can be parallel to the soundboard (e.g., lute, guitar, violin, piano, dulcimer) or at a right angle to the soundboard (e.g., harp).

Woodwind Instruments

Woodwind instruments produce sound through vibrations in an enclosed tube. The vibrations can be set into motion by blowing through single or double reeds, or across or through an opening. **Single-reed** woodwind instruments produce sound when air is blown through a reed that vibrates against the mouthpiece. Single-reed instruments include the clarinet and the saxophone. **Double-reed** woodwind instruments produce sound when air is blown through two reeds that are tied together and vibrate. Double-reed instruments include the oboe, bassoon, and sarrusophone. Woodwinds that produce sound when the player blows across an opening are the transverse flutes, which are held sideways. The whistle and the recorder are woodwinds that produce sound when the player blows directly into an opening. Players change the pitch of an instrument by shortening or lengthening the air column through **covered holes** or **keys**.

Percussion Instruments

Percussion instruments are instruments that produce sound by being hit, scraped, or shaken. Certain percussion instruments such as drums produce sound through the vibration of a membrane around a resonating body. Also known as **membranophones**, the membrane on these instruments can be struck by hands or mallets, as well as rubbed and scraped. Other percussion instruments produce vibrations without the aid of air, string, or membranes; these musical instruments are known as **idiophones** and include concussion idiophones, percussion idiophones, rattles, scrapers, and friction idiophones. Concussion idiophones are two objects that are struck together; examples include rhythm sticks, castanets, and claves. Percussion idiophones are those struck by mallets and include marimbas, bells, gongs, and xylophones. Rattles are shaken, such as a maraca. Scrapers are stroked across a notched surface, such as with washboards and guiros. Friction idiophones are played by rubbing and include the musical saw and the glass harmonica.

Producing Dynamic Changes in Stringed Instruments

On a stringed instrument, many techniques can be applied to produce dynamic changes. When playing with a bow, the variables that affect dynamics are the speed and pressure of the bow. When playing louder dynamics such as forte, fortissimo, and mezzo forte, the bow must move **faster** across the strings with greater pressure to produce greater amplitudes in the vibrating sound waves. When playing softer dynamics such as piano, mezzo piano, and pianissimo, the bow moves a little **slower** across the strings with less pressure to produce smaller amplitudes in the vibrating sound waves. When stringed instruments are **plucked**, this is often notated in the score as pizzicato. When plucking a stringed instrument, the sound produced has a sharper attack; dynamic changes are produced similarly: a heavier pluck at greater speed increases dynamics, while a softer, slower pluck diminishes the dynamics.

Producing Dynamic Changes in Brass Instruments

Dynamics for the brass instruments are a product of the volume of air moving through the instrument, sometimes referred to as **velocity**. Since sound is produced in brass instruments through the buzzing of the player's lips, careful attention must be placed on lip technique when performing dynamic changes, due to the interaction of **embouchure** and the breath. The tendency of a pitch when moving in the direction of piano to forte, if the embouchure remains steady, is for the pitch to bend sharp; it may even move to the next pitch "shelf" due to the increase in velocity. The opposite is also true. At lower dynamic ranges, the player must decrease airflow velocity, which requires additional support through the diaphragm as well as a tighter embouchure, or else the pitch will fall flat.

Dynamic Markings Commonly Used in Music

The dynamic markings commonly used in music come from the written Italian musical tradition of the 17th century. The following markings are in order of increasing loudness. **Pianissimo**, abbreviated *pp*, indicates that the player should play very soft. **Piano**, abbreviated *p*, indicates that the player should play soft. **Mezzo piano**, abbreviated *mp*, indicates that the player should play moderately soft. **Mezzo forte**, abbreviated *mf*, indicates that the player should play moderately loud. **Forte**, abbreviated *f*, indicates that the player should play loud. **Fortissimo**, abbreviated *ff*, indicates that the play should play very loud. Dynamic markings that indicate a gradual change include crescendo and decrescendo or diminuendo. A **crescendo** indicates that the player should play increasingly louder. A **decrescendo** or diminuendo indicates that the player should play increasingly softer.

Sources of Printed and Electronic Information

Encyclopedias and Dictionaries of Music

There are a wide array of authoritative encyclopedias and dictionaries of music, but the following are some exemplary volumes. *The Garland Encyclopedia of World Music* is a 10-volume series of encyclopedic reference material covering all world music. Started in 1988, it is generally regarded as the authoritative source for information regarding ethnomusicology. *The New Grove Dictionary of Music and Musicians*, first published under a different name in 1879, is the authoritative reference work for Western music, with over 20 volumes. *The New Grove Dictionary* is available online through Grove Music Online and is now a part of Oxford Music Online. **Oxford Music Online** is a web resource containing several reference works covering a broad range of musical topics. Online resources through Oxford Music Online include Grove Music Online, The Oxford Dictionary of Music, and The Oxford Companion to Music. *The Encyclopedia of Popular Music*, initiated in 1989 as a popular music counterpart to the definitive *New Grove*, is an authoritative reference work for all popular music, including rock, pop, jazz, hip-hop, reggae, blues, electronica, and heavy metal.

Periodical Databases

Indispensable periodical databases for music history and literature include the following. JSTOR, also known as **Journal Storage**, is a digital database that holds 32 scholarly journals dedicated to music and includes complete back runs of the journals' contents. Titles include *Early Music History, Music Analysis, The Musical Quarterly, Perspectives of New Music*, and *The Journal of Musicology*, among others. **The Music Index Online** is a source for music periodicals and literature from 1973 to the present and contains over 655 international music journals. **The International Index of Music Periodicals** is another important database and indexes over 425 scholarly and popular music periodicals, including *International Journal of Music Education, Ethnomusicology, Jazz Education Journal, Rock and Rap Confidential*, and *Rolling Stone*. For the 19th and 20th centuries, The **Retrospective Index to Music Periodicals** (RIMP) provides a valuable resource for scholarly writing on music history and culture, holding over 200 music periodicals in its database.

Repertoire International des Sources Musicales Online

The Repertoire International des Sources Musicales Online is a musical database founded in Paris in 1952. It is one of the largest non-profit organizations of its kind and operates internationally to document musical sources from around the world. The **RISM** publications are divided into three series. Series A is arranged by composer and includes printed music (Series A/I) and music manuscripts (Series A/II). Series B is arranged by topic, such as ancient Greek music theory or manuscripts in lute tablature. Series C is an index of music libraries, private collections, and archives from around the world. The largest portion of the RISM inventory is Series A/II, consisting of over 380,000 manuscripts by over 18,000 composers, theorists, and librettists from after 1600 AD. The Series A/II is now an online searchable database that lists the composer or author's name, title, origin, and holding library for every entry.

RILM Abstracts of Music Literature

The RILM Abstracts of Music Literature, also known as **Répertoire International de Littérature Musicale**, is an international database focused on scholarship from around the world relating to any aspect of the musical discipline. This includes historical musicology, ethnomusicology, instruments and voice, music therapy, and dance. The international bibliography contains books, catalogs, master's theses, doctoral dissertations, articles, bibliographies, films, videos, ethnographic recordings, conference proceedings, reviews, Festschriften, technical drawings, facsimile editions, and iconographies. The entries are presented in the original language with an English translation of the title, an abstract, and the full bibliographic data. The online searchable database, which covers over 780,000 entries in over 117 languages from 1967 to the present, requires a subscription and is regularly updated.

Critical Listening Skills

Achieving Choral Blend Using Vowel Modification, Dynamics, and Vocal Vibrato

When executing good choral blend, singers must pay attention to their use of vowel modification, dynamics, and vocal vibrato. In a choral setting, **pure vowel** sounds are preferred in producing the sounds a, e, i, o, and u. The mouth cavity must be open with a raised palate to produce the pure vowel sounds. Dynamics among individual singers must be adjusted to compensate for the stronger and weaker singers. When singing in a choral setting, self-monitoring is key in knowing when to adjust sound levels in accordance with the surrounding musicians. Additionally, sections as a whole should adjust their dynamics throughout the performance so that different sections dominate at different times as required by the music. Generally, vocal vibrato should be kept to a minimum when striving for good choral blend; an active vocal vibrato can easily stick out in a choral texture, and works against achieving good choral blend, which should prioritize uniform sound, texture, and tone.

Negative Results of Not Hearing Yourself Sing in a Choral Setting

Spacing within any chorus is of key importance in a healthy choral collaboration. If a singer cannot hear himself or herself, productive collaboration could be hindered and **inaccurate intonation** could become detrimental not only to the individual singer, but also to the group as a whole. If a singer cannot hear himself or herself in a choral setting, then the likelihood of actively listening and constant adjusting to the surrounding musicians becomes minimal; **self-monitoring** is key in productive collaboration. Also, when self-monitoring becomes hindered, then intonation can easily become a problem for the singer. If one singer becomes out of tune in a choral setting, then that voice could easily influence the surrounding singers' intonation, resulting in an entire chorus that becomes out of tune.

Negative Results of Not Hearing Yourself Play in an Ensemble

Self-monitoring within any ensemble is of key importance in a healthy musical collaboration. If an instrumentalist cannot hear himself or herself, **productive collaboration** could be hindered. Inaccurate tuning, rhythm, and phrasing is detrimental not only to the individual instrumentalist, but also to the ensemble as a whole. If an instrumentalist cannot hear himself or herself in an ensemble, then their ability to actively listen and constantly adjust to the surrounding musicians decreases; **self-monitoring** is key in productive collaboration. Also, when self-monitoring becomes hindered, then inaccurate tuning, rhythm, and phrasing can easily become a problem for the instrumentalist. If one instrumentalist in an ensemble becomes out of tune with inaccurate rhythm and phrasing, then that part could easily influence the surrounding musicians' tuning, rhythm, and phrasing, resulting in an entire ensemble with misaligned rhythm and phrasing.

Key Musical Elements of a Unified Ensemble Performance

For a musical ensemble performance to be unified, key musical elements such as tuning, balance, phrasing, articulation, and cut offs must be unified. In any ensemble, **tuning** must be well matched, or else the sound of an out-of-tune ensemble member will noticeably intrude. The **sound intensity** of all the parts must be balanced for a clear melody and support accompaniment to be effective. For example, if the middle ranges of an ensemble are too loud, then the melody of the musical piece will be obscured. **Phrasing** is another important musical element, and if each musician is not phrasing melodies in the same manner, then there is no cohesion in the musical performance. **Articulation** must also be handled in the same way. If some ensemble members play a legato while others play staccato, then the texture of the musical piece becomes muddled. In the same way, if the musicians of an ensemble do not have a simultaneous onset or cutoff of the sound, then the disunity of sound becomes jarringly evident.

Choral Balance vs. Choral Blend

In a choral setting, both choral balance and choral blend are essential elements of a successful and aurally satisfactory choral performance. Both terms refer to the collective sound provided from the group of singers. For a chorus to be balanced, there should be a **choral balance** with an equal level of sound coming from all ranges of voices. If a chorus is not balanced, the term "top-heavy" is used to indicate a sound that has an overabundance of soprano or alto sound, whereas the term "bottom-heavy" is used to indicate a sound that has an overabundance of tenor or bass sound. **Choral blend** refers to the uniformity of vowel formation and tone among the singers. Like choral balance, good choral blend is produced by the collective group; however, uniform choral blend is achieved not by the intensity of each vocal range, but by each individual singer's diligence to the same standard of tone production and blend within the entire chorus.

Notation and Expressive Elements

Elements of Music Needed to Perform a Piece of Music

In order to successfully perform a piece of music, a student must know more than correct notes and rhythm. The student should also analyze all aspects of the melody, rhythm, harmony, and form of the piece. A thorough analysis of the melody, for example, can inform the performer of where the **climax** is, allowing the performer to appropriately time the musical tension and release of the overall piece. Knowing the rhythmic form also allows the performer to note any subtle transitions the composer may be suggesting. The **harmony** of the musical work also holds clues as to the structure of the work, allowing the performer to bring the appropriate mood in transitions and development of the work. The performer should also examine the **historical context** of the piece; knowing the intention and purpose of the composition can inform the musician as to how to execute dynamics, articulations, and releases, depending on the given mood.

How Pitches Are Defined

All clefs indicate the position of a particular pitch on the five-lined staff. The G-clef, the C-clef, and the F-clef are the most common clefs used in modern Western music notation. The **G-clef** spirals around the second line from the bottom, indicating it as the G line for the G pitch above middle C. The **C-clef** has a middle point that is placed to indicate the line as middle C. The C-clef can be placed on the third line, which is typically called the alto or viola clef; when it is placed on the fourth line from the bottom, it is typically called the tenor clef. The **F-clef** looks somewhat like a backwards C with two dots to the right of it; the top point of the curve is placed on the fourth line from the bottom so that the two dots also surround the same line, indicating it as the F pitch below middle C.

Role of Notes, Rests, and Time Signatures

Rhythm is the movement of music over time. As such, certain musical aspects such as pitch duration, silence, and meter play key roles in translating musical symbols to real-time musical rhythm. Pitch durations are notated through note values that sound for a specified time. **Whole notes** are held through four quarter-note lengths. **Half notes** are held for half the length of a whole note. **Quarter notes** are held for half the length of a half note. **Eighth notes** are held for half the length of a quarter note. **Sixteenth notes** are held for half the length of an eighth note, and so forth. Silence durations are notated through rests, which have note name equivalents (e.g., whole notes and whole rests both have durations of four quarter-note length). **Meters** are essential in establishing rhythm, as meters define the general organization of stresses and pulses.

Durational Rhythm vs. Tonal Rhythm

A preliminary study (Schachter 1976) put forward that musical rhythm arises through two separate sources, leading to what Schachter calls tonal rhythm and durational rhythm. **Durational rhythm** is closely tied with meter, and consists of the aspect of rhythm associated with patterns of durations, emphases, and groupings. In contrast, **tonal rhythm** does not arise from patterns of stress and duration, and is essentially independent of meter. It instead arises from rhythmic properties of the tonal system. Example sources of tonal rhythm include recurrence of a single tone, the octave relationship, chordal and linear associations, consonances, and dissonances. It is important to note that any series of tones will have rhythmic characteristics that will be defined by the relative structural importance of the tones, and that duration and structural importance may be unrelated.

Music Terms

The dynamic markings forzando (z), rinforzando (rinf), and sforzando (sfz) all refer to an increased loudness in sound. All three Italian directives have roots from the Italian word *forzare*, which means “to force.” **Forzando**, meaning forced, directs the musician to strongly accent the notes over which the marking occurs. **Rinforzando**, however, has an added prefix and means more precisely “reinforcing” or “strengthening.” The Rinf. dynamic marking usually refers to the increase in volume of a group of notes throughout a phrase and is played increasingly louder similarly to a crescendo but over a shorter length of time. **Sforzando** is most similar to forzando, and the two terms can be interchanged to mean a sudden increase in loudness of the note or notes over which the marking occurs.

Con, translated as “with,” indicates that each of the following terms are descriptions or instructions of a performer's phrasing. **Con amore** translates to "with love," and is equivalent to amorevole or amoroso, "lovingly." Con amore may have multiple correlates within the performance style, translating into a legato articulation, rubato, and more dramatic dynamic contrast. **Con bravura**, similarly, translates to "with bravery" and is a different connotation from bravura as in a bravura performance, which means "skill." Additional terms are **Con brio**, or brioso, "with spirit;" **con fuoco**, "with fire;" **con grazia** "with grace;" **con tenerezza**, "with tenderness." Each term is somewhat subjective; indeed, it may be difficult to establish a clear distinction between con amore, con tenerezza, and con grazia, for example, and they will result in similar interpretations. Con brioso, con fuoco, and con bravura also have many characteristics in common and will differ from an amoroso performance that would have more staccato articulations and limited rubato.

Articulation markings can range from those indicating a shortening of pitch duration to those indicating a lengthening of pitch duration. These articulation markings are presented in decreasing order of duration length: tenuto, portato, staccato, and staccatissimo. **Tenuto**, from the Italian word *tenere* meaning “to hold,” directs the player to hold the note for its full value. In musical notation, a horizontal line over or under the note head marks the tenuto. **Portato**, from the Italian word *portare* meaning “to carry,” directs the player to smoothly detach the notes similarly to a legato, but shorter in length and longer than a staccato. Both dots and a slur over or under the note heads mark the portato. **Staccato**, from the Italian word *staccare* meaning “to detach,” directs the player to shortly detach the note. A dot over or under the note head marks the staccato. **Staccatissimo** is an extremely shortened note and is notated by a wedge or pike above or under the note head.

Tempo markings in order from slowest to fastest are: larghissimo, largo, larghetto, andante, moderato, allegro, vivace, and presto. **Larghissimo** comes from the Italian meaning "very or extremely broad" and should be played very slowly. **Largo** comes from the Italian meaning "broad" and should be played slowly. **Larghetto** is slightly faster than largo. **Andante** comes from the Italian meaning "in a walking manner" and should be played slightly faster than adagio, but slower than moderato. **Moderato** comes from the Italian meaning "moderately" and should be played at an easy comfortable pace. **Allegro** comes from the Italian meaning "fast" and should be played at a quick tempo. **Vivace** comes from the Italian meaning "lively" and should be played faster than allegro but slower than presto. **Presto** comes from the Italian meaning "very fast" and should be played very quickly.

The terms affretando, slentando, allargando, and calando all direct the musician to produce a change in tempo. **Affretando** comes from the Italian word *affretare*, which means "to hurry." When notated within musical notation, affretando indicates a quickening of the tempo and also a character or mood of agitation. **Slentando** means comes from the Italian word *slentare*, which means "to slow down." The player should gradually decrease the tempo of the section as the music slows down. **Allargando** comes from the Italian word *allargare*, which means "to widen." In music, the player should gradually decrease the tempo in a deliberate and imposing character. **Calando** comes from the Italian word *calare*, which means "to let down." Musically, the player should gradually decrease both the tempo and the volume, as calando indicates a mood of calming and dying away.

Bowing Techniques

The **détaché** bowing technique requires the player to detach the notes by playing one note per bow stroke. The **ondulé** technique describes a bow stroke in which the bow plays two adjacent strings like a tremolo. **Sautillé** describes the bouncing of the notes by the middle of the bow that is typically played at a fast tempo. **Sul ponticello** refers to the use of the bow close to the bridge in which a harsh grating sound is produced. **Sul tasto** refers to the use of the bow over the end of the fingerboard to produce a light airy sound. **Martelé** refers to the abrupt release of a stroke in a forceful manner. **Ricochet** refers to the rapid bouncing of the upper third of the bow as the player drops the bow on a down-bow. **Louré** refers to the slight detachment of the notes without changing the direction of the bow. **Col legno** refers to using the stick of the bow on the strings instead of the hair.

Cadenza in the 18th and 19th Centuries

A **cadenza** is described as a section in a large concerto or ensemble work in which the soloist plays without any accompanying instruments. The cadenza may be improvised or written out, but usually occurs at the end of a prominent cadence such as the ending tonic cadence of a movement. The accompanying instruments may pause or play a sustaining note while the soloist continues with the cadenza. In the 18th and 19th centuries, cadenzas became increasingly virtuosic and included more thematic material from the work. Although still commonly improvised, many were increasingly written out by composers as they integrated more complex and elaborate material. Many cadenzas became prescribed instead of merely optional, and they were also placed in increasingly unconventional places within the musical work.

Vocal Timbre

In vocal performance, it is important to express the emotion or mood of the music through **timbre**. Just as vocal expression communicates emotion through regular speech, in music, vocal qualities and inflections help to communicate emotion to the listening audience. Like in speech, to communicate emotions like disgust and loathing, the singer uses a darker timbral quality and may include a raspy delivery and harsher consonants. To communicate emotions like hope and assurance, the singer uses a brighter timbral quality with a smooth, flowing delivery. To communicate emotions like sorrow and gloom, the singer uses a dark and hollow timbral quality and may include a shaky delivery as in regular speech. To communicate emotions like anger and vengeance, the singer uses an intensified dark timbral quality with sonorous delivery of vowels and consonants.

Relationship Between Acoustics and Performance

Physical Properties Behind Sound Production

For sound to be produced, there must be a vibration, or **pressure oscillation,** through a medium that is transmitted through the air and through the mechanical structure of the ear to be perceived as sound in the brain. The source of the oscillation can be any **simple resonator**, which creates fluctuations in the pressure of the surrounding air. The string of a violin, the membrane of a percussion instrument, and the reed of a woodwind instrument all act as resonators. Energy imparted to them through the motion of a bow, the strike of a drumstick, or wind blown across the reed act to set the oscillations in motion. The subsequent physical vibration of the surrounding air travels outwards as complex sound waves. When these sound waves travel to the listener, the membrane of the human eardrum perceives the sound waves and converts the frequencies into aural perception where the listener will hear either a tone or noise.

Pure Tone vs. One Produced By an Instrument

In acoustics, a pure tone is defined as a simple sine wave whose frequency stays constant over time. **Frequency**, measured in Hertz as the number of cycles over time, is perceived by the human ear as pitch. A tone produced by an instrument, however, is not a simple sine wave but is in fact a complex wave; no musical instrument produces a pure tone. When an instrument plays a sound, there is a primary resonating frequency called the **fundamental frequency**, joined by harmonics and overtones as well. The harmonic frequencies resonate at integer multiples of the fundamental and change the overall waveform into a composite waveform. **Pure tones** contain no harmonics or overtones. The various timbres of the different instruments are greatly dependent on the waveform profile of the complex wave.

Role of Resonance

For a singer, resonance plays an important role in enabling the voice to "carry" with a more vibrant and rich sound. Acoustically, the sound originates through the passing of air through the vibrating vocal cords; this movement creates the frequency or pitch that the audience hears. As the sound moves from the vocal cords through the vocal tract, the specific sound properties such as vowels and other resonating properties are created. The vocal tract has **optimal resonances** for certain frequencies, and it is important for the singer to maximize the resonances of the vibrating vocal tract with the specific pitch frequencies. For this reason, many sopranos will maximize vocal tract resonance at high frequencies by creating more space in the oral cavity and relaxing the vocal tract so that the resultant sound is vibrant and sonorous.

Properties of Sound That Contribute to an Instrument's Tone Quality

There are multiple different sound properties that make up an instrument's tone quality. First, an instrument's **tone** is a complex wave that is composed of many different partial frequencies; unlike a simple sine wave that has only the fundamental frequency and no partial frequencies, the sound of a complex wave will vary widely given the profile of the complex wave form, contributing greatly to the various instrumental timbres. Another sound property that affects an instrument's tone quality is the nature of the **resonating body**. Once the vibrations of the instrument are set into motion, the surrounding air will resonate through the instrument's body, whether it be a hollow wooden shell such as a stringed instrument or through a metal tube such a brass instrument. The resonating bodies each have their own unique set of complex resonances known as formants, further giving each instrument its own distinctive tone quality.

Acoustical Implications of Choral Formations

In a **choral blocked** section, the vocal parts are solidly separated from front to back so all sopranos are grouped at one end from front row to back row, altos are grouped next to them from front to back, tenors are grouped next to the altos from front to back, and basses bring up the other end from front to back. The choral sound from a blocked formation tends to be better suited for homophonic pieces, but can create issues of the singers being able to listen to other parts. In a **choral columnar** section, the vocal parts are separated in columns, with tenors behind the sopranos, and basses behind the altos. A column formation suits polyphonic music, as it is easier for singers to hear for balance. In a **mixed formation**, the sopranos, altos, tenors, and basses are individually alternating in SATB pattern. A mixed formation is good for intonation and the mixing of sound at the audience, but may require more training in singing independently.

Acoustical Considerations for Instrumental Ensemble Arrangement

When creating an arrangement for instrumental ensemble formations, there are several key acoustical considerations for the given ensemble to execute the optimal performance. A general guideline holds that softer instruments with important melody lines should sit near the front so that the audience can easily hear their sound. The seating arrangement of the ensemble should ensure that when accompanying parts play softer to balance with the projecting melody, those instruments will not pull back so softly as a deficiency, but they will still be able to support the melody line expressively and imaginatively. Thus, instrument groups with similar lines should be seated together, as well as instrument groups with counter-melodies. This allows the musicians to be more aurally aware of the ensemble and to play with more confidence and freedom.

Rehearsal Room, Concert Hall, Football Field, and Cathedral

A **football field** would have little reverberation time, as the direct signal would already be weakened in the long distances it takes to reach the bleachers as well as the lack of a ceiling to reflect the sound waves. A **rehearsal room** would have slightly more reverberation time, given the presence of a ceiling; the reverberation time of rehearsal rooms vary considerably depending on the wall materials. A **concert hall** would have significantly more reverberation time than a rehearsal room, as the design of the space usually increases the blend of sound and thus reverberation. A **cathedral** would have the most reverberation time of the list, with highly reflective walls typical of these structures and intricate ceilings in which sound waves would have multiples points to reflect and travel.

Reverberation Time

Reverberation time is considered to be the time it takes for sound to decay, usually by 60 decibels from its direct signal. When the direct signal interacts with the materials of a space, some of the energy is absorbed by objects in the space or by absorbent wall materials, while the rest is reflected. As the sound waves bounce off of the various surfaces multiple times, the resultant sound waves are collectively known as **reverberation**; the energy of the sound waves decays over time until there is no energy left to travel. Many factors affect **reverberation time**, including the size of the space, materials within the space, ceiling height, shape of the space, and the amount of people within the space. The longest reverberation times tend to be those of cathedrals and large concert halls, while the shortest reverberation times would be those of open fields or soundproof rehearsal rooms.

Interaction of Reflected Sound with Direct Sound

In an environment other than the theoretical free field where there are no physical objects for sound waves to react to, sound waves undergo reflection, diffraction, and refraction in a performance space. As sound waves leave the source, the energy of the air radiates spherically from the source. This direct sound continues to move outwards until it hits a physical surface. Depending on the absorbency of the physical surface, the sound is either **absorbed** as heat by an absorbent surface, thereby lessening the intensity of the sound, or it is **reflected** by a hard surface, thereby redirecting the direction of the radiating sound waves. As sound waves reflect back toward the source, they create the acoustical phenomenon of reverberation; the listener continues to hear the direct sound followed closely by the reflected sound.

Relationship Between Frequency and Perceived Pitch

Frequency refers to the number of oscillations of a waveform per second, also known as Hertz. **Pitch** is the human perception of the fundamental frequency of a sound wave, and can be affected by distance from the source, amplitude, physiology, and mental expectation. The average human listener can hear frequencies between 16 Hz and ~20,000 Hz. In music, relevant frequencies range from 20 Hz to 5,000 Hz. The range of a guitar, for instance, is from 82 Hz of the lowest E to 330 Hz of the highest E. For the most part, humans hear higher frequencies of oscillations as higher pitches, and lower frequencies of oscillations as lower pitches. Over time, certain frequencies have been standardized for a particular pitch. Concert A, for example, has been measured at 440 Hz since the 20th century.

Perception of Variations in Amplitude

For every sound wave, there are two basic aspects to consider: frequency and amplitude. **Frequency** refers to the number of sound waves per second, also known as Hertz, and is perceived by the human ear as a musical pitch. **Amplitude** refers to the height of the sound wave and is measured in **decibels**. Variations in amplitude are generally perceived by the human ear as changes in loudness; the higher the decibel level, the louder the sound. Variations in amplitude can also be perceived in an attack of a tone. A plucked tone has a sharp attack, and the waveform reaches its peak amplitude quickly, while the amplitude gradually decreases as the sound fades away. Variations in amplitude can also be found in tremolos and vibratos. Although vibratos are generally known as frequency modulation (FM), and tremolos are generally known as amplitude modulation (AM), in execution, both forms of modulation are usually present.

Partials

The concept of partials refers to the specific acoustic property of audible tones. The most basic tone, a pure sine wave, has a frequency that determines the pitch of the wave. In musical sound, however, sound waves are usually much more complex than that of a pure tone, and consist of several different frequencies that become superimposed into one complex sine wave that the human listener perceives as a single tone. The different frequencies of the complex wave are termed **partials** and change the displacement of the combined frequencies. The partial frequencies give the different instruments their unique timbres, as the different components of the sound produced by an oboe, guitar, marimba, glockenspiel, or cymbal superimpose to a unique complex wave configuration of pressure over time.

Overtones

The concept of overtones refers to a specific acoustic property of sound. For every one frequency, there are multiple other frequencies that vibrate through the resonant space through its normal modes. Every instrument has a distinct set of normal modes that vibrate through certain frequencies, giving its timbre and tone. The lowest sounding frequency is termed the **fundamental frequency**; all other frequencies above the fundamental are termed overtones. **Overtones** are partial frequencies and can be harmonic or non-harmonic. **Harmonic overtones** are those that are integral multiples of the fundamental. **Non-harmonic overtones** are those that are not integral multiples of the fundamental. Most musical instruments have overtone frequencies that are near to their harmonic frequencies. Instruments such as brass instruments, gongs, cymbals, and timpani have overtone frequencies that are more distinct from their harmonic frequencies.

Harmonics

The concept of harmonics refers to a specific acoustic property of sound. For every one frequency called the fundamental frequency, there exists a series of other frequencies called the **harmonic set** that are integral multiples of the fundamental: f1, f2, f3, etc. For every fundamental frequency, *f*, the frequency of the nth harmonic is equal to *f* times *n*. The **harmonic frequencies** have acoustically pure tones and most approximate the pitches in standard Western music tuning: the first harmonic occurs an octave above the fundamental; the second harmonic occurs an additional fifth above; the third harmonic occurs an additional fourth above; the fourth occurs an additional third above; etc. The harmonic series helps to define the human perception of pitch; it is so integral, in fact, that humans still perceive the fundamental pitch of the harmonic series even when the fundamental frequency is missing.

Basic Improvisational Techniques and How to Teach Them

Role of Improvisation

Musical creativity holds improvisation at the core of its internal process through the formation of new ideas, sounds, and direction. **Improvisation** is the core vehicle of creativity within the musical realm. A musician might explore musical creativity by utilizing only the black keys on a keyboard; this keeps the tonal context within a simple pentatonic scale and allows the musician to explore various phrases, ideas, and ranges of the keyboard. Improvisation can also foster freer musical creativity through singing or playing along to an existing track. This **structured approach** allows the musician to explore different timbres, harmonies, and tones with freedom. The musician must use mental imagery and mystery when improvising, to conceptualize new and different feelings, moods, and sounds. All of these processes contribute to an overall expansion of a musician's musical creativity and improvisational possibility, leading to more independent melodic, harmonic, and rhythmic improvisation.

Teaching Musical Imitation

Improvisation cannot exist without imitation. As the very basis of improvisation, **imitation** allows students to learn techniques, progressions, melodic contour, and rhythmic patterns from improvisers of the past. Once the student has immersed himself or herself in studying improvisation through imitation, he or she will be much better able to assimilate improvisation techniques for innovation and new musical ideas. Students begin to learn how to imitate from birth. Language acquisition, gestures, and expressions are all learned through imitation. Therefore, as an educator, the process of teaching imitation should focus on musical selection to imitate, allowing the students to explore phrases in various keys and moods. The musical selections should give the students **total immersion** so that the learned framework becomes a launching point for free exploration in the next step toward full improvisation.

Teaching Musical Variation

Much of improvisation consists of variation. Thematic variation, melodic variation, rhythmic variation, stylistic variation, and harmonic variation are all examples of improvisational techniques. When teaching **musical variation** to students, the instructor should begin with only slight variations within a controlled framework. The students may start exploring variation through **melodic variation** first; all other aspects of the music should remain constant so the student has a foundation from which to diverge. Melodies may introduce appoggiaturas, silence, and added neighbor notes, until the melody is so varied that the only recognizable aspects are the constant harmonies. Music educators can also use the **call-and-response** technique for group improvisation, with each call and each response of the students a continued variation of the riff. Educators should incorporate improvisations by students in every concert or project as an extra motivator as students learn how to improvise through techniques such as variation.

Baroque Improvisation vs. Jazz Improvisation

Baroque improvisation and jazz improvisation are separated by more than two centuries of musical development and share widely different origins. **Baroque improvisation** served a primarily religious element in the churches of the time, while **jazz improvisation** was born in the bars and alleyways of New Orleans. Instruments used in Baroque improvisation centered on string instruments, while in jazz improvisation, a wide array of instruments can be found, from brass instruments and voices to drum kits and banjos. However, Baroque and jazz improvisation share many similar traits; although the instrumentations differ, both styles feature a more prominent section as well as a supporting harmonic section. Also, both Baroque and jazz improvisation follow a standard form in performance, whether a 32-bar form in jazz or a ritornello form in Baroque music. Throughout both genres, improvisations are based on outlined chord symbols that direct the melody.

Composing a Harmonic Progression with Proper Root Motion

There are several musical skills necessary for a student to understand in composing a **harmonic progression** with proper root motion. Students should understand the **circle of 5ths** relationship between all 24 diatonic major and minor keys. This systematic organization of keys will help the student in creating key signatures and key relationships within chord progressions. Students should also understand that scales have formulae and spellings, and whole and half tones, as well as understand the concept of **diatonic harmony**. Without these precursory concepts, the student will have a harder time grasping the basic diatonic harmony of a major scale with Roman numeral designations. Students should also understand all inversions of triads and seventh chords, as the composition of proper root motion assumes the incorporation of appropriate inverted chords. Also important in the composition of harmonic progressions is proper voice leading of all four SATB voices, which in turn informs the proper motion of the chord roots.

Technologies Used for Performance and Recording Production

Mechanisms of a Simple Sound System

A simple sound system used for sound amplification consists of an input transducer, signal processing, and an output transducer. One type of **input transducer** is a microphone, which converts the sound that is picked up into audio signals that travel down cables to the signal processor. A **signal processor** takes the form of a mixing console through which the audio signals are processed in three ways. First, the audio signal goes through a preamplification system in which the sound that is picked up is amplified to line level. Then, the audio signal goes through an equalizer in which an audio engineer or console operator adjusts the specific levels of tone quality for the most aesthetically pleasing balance. If necessary, the audio signal undergoes mixing, in which multiple inputs are processed together into one line-level output signal. The single line-level output signal is then amplified and converted back into sound through an **output transducer**, such as a loudspeaker.

Proper Microphone Technique for Vocal Amplification

When singing into a microphone, a singer may have immaculate vocal technique but still not sound ideal. **Vocal amplification** requires proper microphone technique to maximize the aesthetic balance of a loudspeaker. A good sound starts with an ideal fit between the voice and the microphone. A high-pitched voice would fit with a microphone that adds warmth through the mid and low ranges, whereas a deeper and darker voice would fit better with a microphone that lightens the sound with treble and upper-mid prominence. Also, the singer should sing into the **center** of the microphone, not across the top or at a wrong angle. The singer should not strain to sing into the microphone, but should think of the microphone as an extension of the ears. Singers should sing at a consistent distance away from the microphone to ensure maximal sound pick-up. If there is a sudden increase in singing volume, however, the singer should back away slightly so as not to blast the sound system.

MIDI Technology

MIDI stands for **Musical Instrument Digital Interface** and provides a standard "language" of MIDI that allows communication between digital keyboards, computers, and even cell phones. MIDI does not record a digital version of a sound recording, but instead stores performance data of a particular performance. MIDI data includes tempo settings, which notes are to be played, what rhythms are to be played, which instruments are to be played, and the volume levels of the instruments. Since the recorded data are inherently performance instructions, MIDI-stored performances can be changed to sound on different instruments, in different keys, and in different tempi. MIDI technology has become a staple in the music industry, with its simplicity of recording, compact storage size, and multitude of practical applications in recording, editing, and performing.

DAW

DAW stands for **Digital Audio Workstation** and is a computer-based recording, sequencing, and mixing tool for the modern musician. A complete DAW includes the computer, the digital audio software, a digital audio interface, optional plug-ins, digital signal processing, and possibly additional digital audio interfaces. It is important to choose the right digital sequencing software to have the right tools where needed. **Avid Pro Tools** is a popular DAW software and has become the standard in recording studios and home studios as well. **MOTU Digital Performer** is one of the oldest DAWs around and is compatible with both Mac and Windows. **Apple Logic Pro** is also one of the top DAWs and provides a wealth of interface options, but it is only compatible with Apple products. **Ableton Live** is one of the best live recording DAWs and offers many third-party hardware options made especially for the program. **FL Studio** is a classic DAW for creating loop- and sample-based music.

Classroom Computer for Music Use

A classroom computer in any music room proves to be an invaluable resource for the 21st century music student. With the music technology at hand, a classroom computer can help to reinforce lesson materials, provide a launching pad for music technology instruction, and offer students a wide array of resources for making music. The classroom computer should have enough RAM and storage to run multimedia programs, be Internet-ready, and have audio input and output features, speakers, and a CD- or DVD-ROM player. The computer should have easy-to-use menu screens and controls so that the students can easily navigate through the programs. The computer should have loudspeakers as well as headphones. The computer should also include MIDI, notation, and sequencing software, as well as electronic instruments with which to experiment and create sound in the DAW software.

Notation Software

Notation software provides an important tool in music education, allowing students to notate compositions electronically, transfer the data to other MIDI instruments, and integrate technology into the music classroom. Using **notation software** helps to reinforce musical concepts and compositional lessons for the students. Many notation programs will transcribe the music as it is played on an attached keyboard or sung into a microphone. Notes can also be manually input by the mouse. The premier notation software **Sibelius** features high ease of use, varied input/output capabilities, great editing options, and good technical support. **Finale** is another widely used notation software and features both student and professional versions. **MagicScore Maestro** features easy notational input, but does not have controls that are as intuitive as other notation software. **Forte Home** is a great notation software for the beginner but features no virtual piano.

Inputting Music into Desktop Music Publishing Software

There are various methods of inputting music into desktop music publishing software. Many programs will notate the music as played by a **MIDI instrument** such as a keyboard or guitar. Some programs can also notate music that is **sung** into a microphone. This method allows the most organic processing from live music to notation, but may require some cleaning up after the music has been notated into the program. Another way of inputting music into desktop music publishing software is by **manually placing** each note and rest through the mouse. This method allows for more meticulous control of each note placement, but can be highly time-consuming. Some desktop music publishing software can process **scanned print music** into the proper notational format within the software. This method is highly efficient for multiple pages of sheet music, but will still have to be cleaned once the scanned music has been transferred into the program.

Finale, Nightingale, and Overture

Finale is one of the most widely used notation software packages on the market. It allows music to be input through MIDI-controlled instruments as well as through scanning, and then converts the data onto a staff. Finale features a diverse playback instrument library and allows easy sharing between users. Tools like transposition, range checking, production, and sequencing capabilities make Finale an essential tool for the musician. **Nightingale** notation software is available on the Mac platform only, and offers a simple, basic approach to digital notation. Nightingale offers a PostScript output equal to that of other notation software, with similar features such as MIDI and scanning input, as well as playback, transposition, and orchestration tools. **Overture** is highly intuitive notation software that features many similar tools such as both MIDI and scanning input, along with diverse editing options, but it also includes VST, Virtual Studio Technology, which allows ease of integration between software audio synthesizers, plug-ins, Overture, and other recording systems.

Filtering Software for Music Classrooms

Filtering software is one method to protect students from obscene, inappropriate, and otherwise harmful websites on the Internet. The **filtering software** can be set to a variety of levels, from most restrictive to least restrictive. Even at the least restrictive setting, the software blocks pornographic content, obscene subject matter, and other inappropriate websites. The more restrictive settings marginally block more content, but may also block safe educational content through unreliable and inconsistent measures. Some educators have voiced opposition to filtering software, due to the inconsistent and unreliable results, interference of legitimate education websites, and a lack of input across the school district. Opposition also claims that filtering software prevents students from learning how to make their own sound decisions based on real-world knowledge. Despite the challenges of filtering software, it is still a necessary tool in providing a safe and positive learning environment for students.

Music License

Under the 1976 Copyright Act, music teachers are exempt from copyright recording laws only if they make a single copy of a student performance of a copyrighted work for educational purposes or for documentation. If a teacher makes **duplicates** of the recording, then a music license is necessary. In this case, a **licensing fee** is required for each copy of the recording that is duplicated and distributed. Music educators must contact the Harry Fox Agency to acquire the correct music license for distribution. The licensing fee applies to each copyrighted work. Although festivals and recording companies may pay royalty fees, it is ultimately the music educator's responsibility to ensure that all royalties are paid to prevent undue consequences from copyright law enforcement.

Common Performance Challenges and their Causes

Instructional Activities

Improving Rhythmic Accuracy in Beginner Students

Many times, rhythmic inaccuracy in beginner students results from a lack of basic reinforcement of the concept of a steady beat. Beginner music students will benefit from heavy **reinforcement** of a steady beat through movement activities such as dancing to the beat of a song, clapping or tapping along to a rhyme, swaying back and forth while counting out loud, or other forms of **multi-sensory learning** that involve the kinesthetic mode as well as the aural mode. Beginner music students will also benefit from visual and aural modeling from the music educator as well as from peers. **Peer learning** can be a great source of motivation and encouragement to learn, as students will generally want to match the level of their peers. Music educators should also introduce the concept of the **heartbeat** in practicing a steady beat, relating the abstract concept of tempo and meter to a familiar one of the body.

Improving Pitch Reading in Beginner Students

Pitch reading can be a challenging concept for beginner students, as many mental processes occur from the written visual cue to the symbolic processing, to knowledge retrieval, to the answering output. For beginner students, it is important to have a **reference** when pitch reading, whether it is middle C or another referential pitch. Students should also understand the **spatial relationships** required in note reading, that higher on the staff also means higher in pitch and that lower on the staff also means lower in pitch. The music educator should ensure that the beginner student understands how to play high and low on his or her respective instrument before continuing the lessons into more complex playing. Similarly to language learning, the music educator should also provide ample **reinforcement** and practice in pitch reading as the student begins to integrate the musical symbols with aural and pitch meaning.

Rote Learning Vs. Intervallic Note Reading

The rote method of note reading refers to teaching a student to read notes from memory. Techniques to teach students to read by rote include **mnemonic devices** such as the lines of the treble clef ("Every Good Boy Does Fine"), the spaces of the treble clef ("FACE"), the lines of the bass clef ("Good Boys Do Fine Always"), and the spaces of the bass clef ("All Cows Eat Grass"). **Intervallic note reading** refers to the method of reading by intervallic relationships (e.g., a third up, a second down, a fourth up). Intervallic note reading relies on spatial visualization, while rote reading relies on memorization. While both methods of note reading result in proficient musical skills, pros and cons exist for each. In rote reading, students are more quickly able to identify note names; however, sight-reading may be slightly slower because of the added mental processing of labels. In intervallic reading, students are more quickly able to identify direction and intervals during sight-reading; however, note naming may be slightly more difficult as students must first process intervals.

Pyramid Model of Balance and Blend

The pyramid model of balance and blend refers to the theory that higher-pitched singers and instruments should play softer than the lowest-pitched singers and instruments, so that an ideal **balance** exists between the treble and the bass. In this model, the-higher pitched section will also be able to hear the bass for better intonation and blend. In the **pyramid model**, the bass voices and instruments constitute the bottom rung of the pyramid; the width of the pyramid determines the overall volume of the ensemble. As the pyramid rises, higher-pitched voices and instruments are stacked above the bass section to the tip of the pyramid where the highest treble section is placed. The higher the voice or instrument is on the pyramid, the softer the sound should be. To apply it to an ensemble, the director should have the bass section play or sing a fortissimo, the tenor section a forte, the alto section a mezzo-forte, and the soprano section a mezzo-piano, so that the full ensemble can experience the balance and blend of the pyramid model.

Bright Tone vs. Dark Tone

"Bright" and "dark" are descriptions of tonal quality. **Tonal quality** is independent from pitch, as demonstrated by a violin and a cello. If both were played to produce the same note, their tonal qualities would still differ, with the violin producing a brighter tone. A **bright tone** emphasizes the partials in the upper midrange. A **dark tone**, in contrast, will have a tonal balance emphasizing the lower range, with weak high frequencies. In terms of singing, a bright tone is one that resonates farther forward in the face, and is associated with the front vowels [i] and [e]. A dark tone resonates further back, and is associated with the vowels [u], [o], and [a]. In a full chorus, the brightness or darkness of a passage can be adjusted through the manipulation of vowel quality. In general, female vocalists will tend to have brighter tones.

Improving Chorus' Intonation and Vocal Technique

A fundamental element of good choral sound lies in accurate intonation. Without all of the voices sounding in pitch, balance and blend become the least of a choral director's concerns. There are many rehearsal techniques to improve a chorus' intonation. Sometimes, changing the **seating arrangement** of the chorus can drastically improve intonation. Be sure that all vocal parts can hear each other clearly so that intonation is no longer an issue. If the seating arrangement is not the issue, then the director can take the singers through a problem spot singing every beat **vertically**, stopping on each harmony for accurate pitches. Directors can also warm up with dominant chords and tonic pedals so that the singers always have a **reference pitch** to tune to. Singers should practice breathing exercises, vocalizations, and etudes to strengthen their vocal mechanisms and their overall vocal technique.

Correcting Intonation

Brass Instruments

Correct intonation on brass instruments is the result of properly forming the entire system flowing from the diaphragm to the end of the instrument. Playing with good posture and breath support allows the player to play at a wide variety of registers and volumes more comfortably, reducing strained intonation that can occur at extremes. Cue the student to think of the airway from the lungs to the throat and the oral cavity as a broad and open passageway. Playing in front of a **mirror** allows the student to monitor horn placement and embouchure. **Mental practice** is extremely important; the student should have a clear idea of the tone to produce and think actively about playing with good tone. **Long tones** are an excellent tool for developing intonation. Depending on the particular instrument, the student should learn which note fingerings are inherently out of tune and how to adjust the relevant slide to compensate.

Woodwind Instruments

Correct intonation on woodwind instruments is the result of properly forming the entire system flowing from the diaphragm to the end of the instrument. Playing with good posture and breath support allows the player to play at a wide variety of registers and volumes more comfortably. Cue the student to think of the airway from the lungs to the throat and the oral cavity as a broad and open passageway. Playing in front of a mirror allows the student to monitor **embouchure**. The student should have a clear idea of the tone she wants to produce, while thinking actively about playing with good tone. Long tones are an excellent tool for developing intonation. **Tuning** to the rest of the ensemble, piano, or tuner should be done only after a thorough warm-up, at which point tuning adjustments to the instrument, such as pushing in or pulling out sections, can be made.

Ensemble Rehearsal Strategies

During an ensemble rehearsal, there are many rehearsal strategies to take on technically challenging passages. The music director should first determine if the technically challenging passage is the result of a lack of **individual practice**. If so, the director should show the students in detail the correct way to practice individually and at home. If the passage still presents technical challenges for the ensemble, the music director should take the ensemble through the passage **slowly and rhythmically** to identify the probable origin of the difficulty. Then the educator will be able to assist the ensemble in note accuracy, technical facility, and fluency in playing. Once the ensemble has the tools to fix the challenging passage, the ensemble should go through the passage again slowly in **isolation** and then slowly speed up the challenging passage until performance tempo has been reached. The ensemble should practice scales, arpeggios, and technical etudes to further develop technical skills.

Fostering a Relaxed Instrumental Playing Approach

Approaching instrumental playing in a healthy manner requires a relaxed body to prevent injuries and to enhance instrumental tone and resonance. **Physical tension** in a musician can translate into an unpleasant, thinner, and pinched sound. Music educators can foster a relaxed approach to instrumental playing through daily instructional activities that encourage flexibility and freedom at the instrument. Rehearsals and music classes that start with **physical stretching** help students to release any existing tension, while signaling to the body a time for increased blood flow and loose joints. Music educators can implement warm-ups that involve tensing and releasing the shoulders so students can feel the presence and absence of tension in their bodies. Consistent and frequent reminders for a student to relax any tension will also help to make a relaxed approach a habit for the student.

Role of the Tongue in Forming Clear Diction and Vowel Formation

The tongue plays a key role in vowel formation and clear diction, as it directly influences the vocal tract and the larynx. With all other vocal mechanisms fixed, a change in the **tongue** directly changes the vocal sound, from dull and distorted to tinny and harsh. Clarity in singing requires clear vowel formation for the words to be intelligible to the listening audience. For **clear vowels**, the tongue should rest forward in the mouth, with the tip of the tongue resting against the bottom teeth for the most space in the mouth for resonance. The back of the tongue should not press against the throat, but should be kept away from the throat for clear and unobstructed delivery of airflow and sound. The tongue should always be kept relaxed and free from tension when singing, to avoid a choked sound and possible injury to the vocal mechanisms.

Programming a Widely Diverse Repertoire for an Ensemble

Diversity of repertoire is an important and current topic for music directors in the present era of concert programming. Good concert programming will reflect the **diversity** that the audience experiences in the world around them. Concerts must engage the audience with relevant and fresh perspectives through new and culturally diverse works as well as through the musical standards of the past. Showcasing contemporary, newer works alongside a traditional classical work can inform and rejuvenate the audience's listening ear. Programming new works along with old works also illuminates the performance practices of the past, where Beethoven and Wagner both featured works of their present along with the past. Students will have a broader **musical perspective** by experiencing music from different cultures, genres, and time periods. Widely diverse concert programs can unite audience members of the past, of today, and of the future.

Differences in Concert Length

A concert planned for a beginning middle school band will differ widely from a concert planned for an advanced high school concert band. The beginning middle school band will have had little experience with performances and may still be working through rudimentary techniques and skills on their instruments. Repertoire for the beginning middle school band will focus mostly on easily accessible beginner works. The advanced high school concert band, however, will have at least a few years of experience performing and playing their instruments. Repertoire selection for the advanced concert band will have a wider range of intermediate to advanced works. **Endurance** is also an issue for the beginning band; concert length will be shorter, with shorter musical works and more frequent changes. The advanced high school band will be able to perform longer works of music with less frequent breaks.

Fixed-Do System vs. Movable-Do System

In the **fixed-do system** of notational reading, the solmization of pitches refers to a specific pitch, usually where *do* refers to the C pitch, *re* refers to the D pitch, *mi* refers to the E pitch, and so on. In the **movable-do system** of notational reading, the solmization of pitches refers to any pitch within a diatonic scale so that *do* refers to the tonic, *re* refers to the supertonic, *mi* refers to the mediant, and so on. In the movable-do system, any pitch can be *do*, while the rest of the diatonic scale is built upon the relative tonic pitch. The fixed-do system of notational reading focuses on the functional association of the specific pitches to the staff, where *do* is always recognized as C. The movable-do system of notational reading focuses on the intervallic relationship between the pitches as they occur within the scale.

Incorporate Solfege into Regular Rehearsals

When teaching an ensemble how to sight-read, it is useful to incorporate **solfege** into rehearsals to teach the relative relationship between pitches as they occur within any diatonic scale. The reinforcement of solfege on a movable-do system trains the student's understanding of **relative pitch**. As the students learn to sight-read through solfege, they will be able to identify the relative position of the pitch within a scale, without the additional processing of identifying the absolute pitch. Music educators should begin by teaching students all the solfege syllables, with the added hand motions that reinforce the spatial relationships between pitches. The solfege syllables should be reinforced by singing through a number of different keys to train the student's ears to hear the relationships between the diatonic pitches. As the lessons progress, students should be required to sing or play back certain pitch intervals in various keys, such as a do-mi-sol progression.

Kinesthetic Theories of Rhythm Reading

The kinesthetic theories of rhythm reading hold that rhythm cannot be experienced without having first experienced its movement physically. Since rhythm refers to the flow of movement through space, students should experience rhythm through their bodies first. Once the rhythm has been experienced physically through movement, students will more readily be able to audiate the rhythm mentally during rhythm reading. Phyllis Weikart, a prominent figure in movement pedagogy, advocated the introduction of **movement-based learning** in early childhood education, so that early gross motor development could better prepare students for more complex rhythmic integration in musical development. Other motor theorists also found that rudimentary motor movements are formed before the age of five, and all other motor movements after the age of five are reinforcements and stabilizations of those fundamental motor movements learned in early childhood.

Instructional Activities That Aid Intervallic Reading and Understanding

Intervallic reading is founded on the principle that students who can recognize the relative relationships between pitches will be able to read more quickly and with less **mental processing** demands than reading note by note. Students who read music note by note must first mentally identify the pitch name, translate that into the fingering or key pattern on the instrument, and then play. Students who read intervallically can forgo the pitch identification step of mental processing and proceed immediately to spatial processing, thus **simplifying** the reading process. Music educators can use instructional activities that reinforce the concept of spatial distance and direction, such as dictating a tune by note distance and direction only (e.g., 2nd up, 3rd down), making a game out of flash cards, being able to play intervals and directions with eyes closed, and practicing placing notes on a classroom staff.

Neural Bases for Mental Practice Efficacy

Mental practice has been shown to be a highly effective method of instrumental practicing when access to an instrument is not possible. When musicians practice traditionally on an instrument, the maxim "practice makes perfect" describes the correct pattern-forming process of the brain. Many music educators ascribe instead to the phrase "practice makes permanent," as scientists now know that repeated practicing **reinforces** the cognitive neural pathway of a particular action, similarly to the way habits are formed. It is therefore important for a musician to make sure to practice passages correctly, or else incorrect technique can easily be habituated by repeated practicing. The concept for **mental practicing** mirrors the neural processes of physical practice, and helps to reinforce a particular neural pathway even without movement. Mental practice combined with physical practice provides optimal cognitive and motor learning for a musician.

Characteristics of the Reed That Influence Intonation

The reed interacts with the player's airflow and vibrations against the body of the instrument in four ways that influence the tone and sound. A reed's **response** refers to the ability of the reed to maintain a high quality of sound through all registers without splattering or spreading. The reed's **resistance** refers to the amount of embouchure tension required to keep the reed behaving and sounding with a good tone. A reed that has a low resistance may cause the player to overblow in searching for a fuller tone, while a reed that has a high resistance can cause the player fatigue and difficulty in creating a good tone. A reed's **tone quality** refers to the resonance and timbre of the reed itself. A reed with only lower partials will sound dull; a reed with only higher partials will sound shrill and thin. A reed's **stability** refers to the ability of the reed to hold pitch at any dynamic and can influence the sound (e.g., sounding flat, stable, wild, sharp, or dull).

Woodwind Embouchure

There are two types of woodwind embouchure based on the type of woodwind in question; **transverse flute embouchures** require the player to blow air across the instrument body, while the **reed woodwind embouchure** requires the player to enclose the mouthpiece so that the airflow can effectively vibrate the reed in sound production. The transverse flute should be placed against the chin so that the bottom lip is in line and close to the hole. The corners of the mouth should be relaxed, while the upper lip is held firmly against the upper teeth. On a reed woodwind, the mouthpiece should be taken into the mouth only as far as the reed meets the mouthpiece. The bottom lip should be placed slightly over the bottom teeth and against the reed. The upper teeth should rest on top of the mouthpiece while the corners of the mouth are drawn in to create a seal around the mouthpiece.

Bow Position and Bow Handling

The bow position on a **violin and viola** should have a rounded thumb holding the side of the bow with a pinky on top of the bow, with the other fingers comfortably holding the other side of the bow. The fingers should be fairly arched during a down stroke and more elongated during an up stroke. The bow should not be held with any tension, but firmly and lightly. The player should be careful not to extend any finger, as this will create tension in the wrist. On the **cello and bass**, the bow should be held in a similar manner to both the violin and viola bow, but the pinky finger does not rest on top of the bow; instead, the pinky should rest next to the middle and ring fingers. Since both the cello and bass are played upright, the arm does not generally stay above the bow; in fact, bow handling on a cello and bass requires the elbow and arm to lower significantly whether playing near the tip of the bow or near the frog.

Mutes and Resulting Sounds for Trumpets and Trombones

The trumpet and trombone share all the most popular mutes, with a trumpet and trombone version of each of the straight mute, cup mute, bucket mute, wah-wah mute, plunger, and hat. The difference between a trumpet mute and one for trombone is principally one of scale. The **straight mute** results in a tinny, metallic sound. The **cup mute** produces a muffled, darker tone and was common in trumpet sections during the classic big band era of the 1930s and 1940s. The **bucket mute** produces a softer tone and reduces the piercing quality of loud or high notes that can be amplified by other mutes. The **wah-wah mute**, often known by the brand-name Harmon mute, produces a buzzed tone, and for trumpet is often associated with Miles Davis during his cool jazz period. The **plunger** and the **hat mute** are used similarly, with the musician playing with one hand while manipulating the mute over the front of the bell with the other.

Hand-Horn Technique for French Horn

Hand-horn technique, also known as right-hand technique, is the placing of the right hand inside the **bell** of the horn. The technique was derived from early versions of the instrument, which had no valves. In these instruments, notes between the open partials of the harmonic series were played by opening and closing the throat of the bell with the hand. When valves were added, horn players still played with the **right hand** inside the bell in order to produce a slightly darker tone, more easily control pitch, and perform extended techniques such as stopped horn and echo horn. There are two methods for hand placement inside the bell. In the **American method**, the hand is held flat with the metal touching the back of the hand, with some of the horn's weight supported by the thumb. In the **French method**, the right hand is held out flat with palm down and the thumb forming a 90-degree angle with the hand, and some of the horn's weight is supported by the first knuckles and the back of the hand.

Multiple Mallet Techniques Used by Marimba Players

Good mallet technique for marimba players allows the musicians a free range of color and technical possibilities, and starts with one mallet in each hand. Once the **two-mallet grip** has been learned with a flexible grip, the student usually learns the **four-mallet grip** next. The three main multiple mallet grips are the traditional crossed grip, the Burton grip, and the Musser/Stevens grip. The **traditional grip** places the second mallet between the index and middle fingers while grasping the end of the second mallet with the ring finger and pinky. The traditional grip has a higher rate of tension and less support than the other grips. The **Burton grip** places the second mallet between the index and middle fingers and the end of the mallet underneath all four fingers. The **Musser/Stevens grip** places the first mallet between the thumb and index fingers, and the second mallet between the middle and ring fingers so that the mallets are not crossed. The Musser/Stevens grip provides the most independence of mallet movement.

Proper Body, Arm, and Finger Position for Snare Drum

To execute proper snare drum technique, full attention must be made to develop the body, arm, and finger position of the player. The **body** should be in a fully relaxed and comfortable position without allowing the back to slouch or lean in. A seated body position in playing the snare drum should allow the feet to be flat on the floor with the legs spread evenly. The drum set should always be positioned to the player so that the player does not have to adjust unnaturally to the set. The player should be seated facing directly in front of the snare drum and not to the side or from below. The **arms** should always be relaxed and should hang at the body's side without unnecessary tension. The snare player should **grip** the drumstick firmly and in a relaxed manner so that each stroke has a flowing yet controlled movement with a full, legato sound.

Fingering Techniques for Keyboard Instruments

When executing finger technique on keyboard instruments, one must always be aware of relaxed wrists, arms, elbows, and shoulders to prevent overuse injuries. The **wrist** should be held in line with the hand and the arm, not sagging or raised too high. The **elbows** should hang comfortably to the side of the body and never tensed. The **shoulders** should be relaxed and dropped; raised shoulders are a sign of tension. **Fingering** at the keyboard should use the thumb-tuck technique, to allow a flowing and continuous line of notes when playing. When tucking the thumb under the middle or ring fingers, the keyboardist should ensure that the wrist does not drop during the movement, but that the thumb helps to maintain a healthy wrist position. Players should always drill a fingering section slowly at first, and they should only increase the playing speed if the passage can be executed without tension.

Kinesthetics of Octave Playing on Keyboard Instruments

When the keyboardist plays an octave passage in either or both hands, the hand is required to **stretch** to the length of eight keys. The motion should be played and released quickly since the reach of the octave can present unnecessary tension and exhaustion to the arm if not released quickly. One school of thought has the hand play an octave quickly, then releasing the **tension** as quickly as possible back to a neutral hand position. In a long passage of octave playing, this method requires the quick stretch and release at each octave. Another school of thought has the hand fixed in an octave position and uses the quick movement of a flexible **wrist snapping** for each motion to play the octave passage as quickly as possible. Yet another school of thought has the hand and wrist fixed in the octave position and uses the quick movement of the **elbow** to play each octave.

Importance of the Diaphragm in Breathing for Vocal Music

The diaphragm plays a central role in the respiratory system, as one of the main acting forces behind inhalation and exhalation. The **diaphragm** is a sheet of muscle that separates the abdomen from the chest cavity. The diaphragm muscle is attached to the lower parts of the rib cage, the spine, and the lower edge of the sternum. As the muscle contracts, it increases the length and diameter of the chest cavity, causing a vacuum in the lungs, inducing air to enter the lungs through **inhalation**. During **exhalation**, the diaphragm muscle naturally relaxes, deflating the lungs and expelling the air out from the lungs. When singing, it is important to actively engage the diaphragm during inhalation for a deep supported breath, as well as during exhalation to prolong the supported singing breath as long as possible.

Adolescent Vocal Change

As students undergo puberty, hormonal fluctuations and growth spurts many singers experience the added challenges of **adolescent vocal change**. Females typically undergo puberty between the ages of 10 and18, while males typically undergo puberty between the ages of 12 and 20. Adolescent vocal change occurs in both males and females, but it is most prominent in male singers. During puberty, the vocal tract increases in length and circumference, and the larynx increases in size and density. Symptoms include cracking and abrupt register breaks. While the vocal mechanisms are developing in adolescent students, it is important to practice safe and intelligent techniques of singing rather than pushing the vocal mechanisms to damage. The body should be both energetic and relaxed, providing proper support for the breath but never pushing. Equally important during this developmental stage is proper **rest** for the singing voice; students should never sing too loud or with too much effort, which could injure the vocal mechanisms.

Tessitura

Tessitura refers to that range within a singer's vocal abilities that resonate the most in an aesthetically pleasing manner. The particular **tessitura** of a singer's voice type is also usually the most comfortable for his or her vocal timbre. Tessitura differs from vocal range in that the range of a singer's voice refers to the limits of pitches the singer is able to sing; the tessitura of a singer's voice, although he or she may have a wide singing range, may be best described as a high tessitura, or a low tessitura, wherever the voice is able to sustain the most dramatic, comfortable, and pleasing sound. When assigning a singer's voice to a vocal part, it is important to consider the tessitura of that particular voice as well as his or her range, timbre, transition points, and voice weight.

Chapter Quiz

Ready to see how well you retained what you just read? Scan the QR code to go directly to the chapter quiz interface for this study guide. If you're using a computer, simply visit the online resources page at **mometrix.com/resources719/nesincmusic** and click the Chapter Quizzes link.

Music History, Literature, and Culture

Music History and Literature

Characteristics of Music in the Medieval Era

Music of the Middle Ages (~500–1400 AD) was dominated by vocal music that could be separated into two separate genres. **Sacred music** included Gregorian chant and masses, and **secular music** included music for dance and entertainment, such as that of the troubadours and trouvères. **Gregorian chant** had melodies that were free flowing with no distinct meter, melismatic, and largely monophonic, sung by unaccompanied voice or choir. The sacred music of the Middle Ages evolved with the development of organum, an early form of polyphony in which voices were sung in parallel motion. Masses were also an important religious ritual and featured non-imitative polyphony. The most important form of Medieval polyphony was the **motet**, which was introduced in the 13th century and spanned both sacred and secular genres. By the end of the Middle Ages, secular music became the driving force of musical development, and the music of troubadours and trouvères saw drone accompaniment and had regular meter, syncopations, polyphony, and harmony.

Musical Importance of the Mass

As one of the most important services of the Roman Catholic Church, the **mass** was a driving force of musical development in the Medieval and Renaissance eras. **The liturgy of the Ordinary** was most often set to music, and musical advancements were applied to the composition of the mass. By the Renaissance era (~1400–1600 AD), polyphony was common, musical notation had been refined, and complete masses were written by a single composer. The first mass by a known composer was the *Messe de Notre Dame* written by Guillaume de Machaut in the 1360s. As a large-scale form, the mass continued to appear in the oeuvres of many composers, including that of Dufay, Josquin, Palestrina, Haydn, Mozart, Beethoven, Schubert, Weber, Berlioz, Verdi, Wagner, Fauré, and others. Although the genre declined through the 20th century, composers continue to set the mass to new musical settings (Hindemith, Stravinsky, Bernstein, etc.) The Ordinary includes six sections and is outlined as follows: Kyrie, Gloria, Credo, Sanctus, Benedictus, and Agnus Dei.

Medieval Motet vs. Renaissance Motet

The motet was a major musical form of the Medieval and Renaissance periods that emerged from medieval organum and clausulae. The **Medieval motet** featured a tenor line derived from plainchant with one or more upper voices in French or Latin. The tenor vocal line usually had a short, repeated rhythmic pattern, while the upper voices had contrasting, lively melodic lines. The texts of the upper voices were sometimes independent and in a different language from the tenor line. The **Renaissance motet**, in contrast, referred more to a genre of music than to a certain form or structure. By the mid-15th century, the motet was known as a polyphonic setting of any sacred Latin text, not restricted to the liturgy. Composers of the Renaissance introduced imitation, homophony, and four-part harmony to the motet.

Polyphony, Homophony, and Monophony

The terms polyphony, homophony, and monophony all refer to a certain texture of music. **Polyphony** refers to a texture of music in which all voices or parts hold similar musical prominence or interest. This can be thought of as several distinct melodic lines occurring at the same time. The rhythm of each line in polyphonic music moves independently of each other line. **Homophony** also has several voices or parts, but melodic interest is reduced to a single voice or part. All other voices or parts support the main melody as accompaniment and move together in rhythmic likeness. In this way, homophony can be thought of as any form of melody and accompaniment texture. **Monophony** also centers on a single melodic line; however, unlike homophony, it does not have supplemental accompaniment parts. A prime example of monophony is plainchant in which a single line of melody embodies the entire work itself.

CRITIQUES OF BAROQUE MUSIC BY CLASSICAL COMPOSERS

In the **Baroque** era (~1600–1750 AD), music was stylistically ornate and heavily ornamented. During this period, tonality was established, counterpoint was invented, and the size, range, and complexity of orchestrations were expanded. By the end of the Baroque era, music innovations became so complex that a new aesthetic was formed in reaction against the overly embellished Baroque aesthetic. Homophony replaced polyphony, simplicity replaced complexity, and gentler sentiment replaced strong passion. With the prominence of homophony, music of the **Classical** era (~1750–1830 AD) featured a slower harmonic rhythm than the ornate Baroque music, which normally featured a linear bass line. Classical composers emphasized a natural melody above textural complexity and wrote music with a clear phrase and period structure. Instead of keeping a musical piece in one affect as in the Baroque period, Classical composers introduced stylistic contrasts within a piece.

NATIONALISM

The Nationalist movement was a facet of the Romantic era during the late 19th and early 20th centuries in which music evoked the national or regional character of a place. Composers used folk music in their compositions either as a direct quote or as a framework for the composition of melodies and rhythms that resemble folk music of the area. Nationalistic composers who represented Russia include Glinka, Borodin, Balakirev, Mussorgsky, and Rimsky-Korsakov. Nationalistic composers who represented Czechoslovakia include Smetana, Dvořák, and Janáček. Composers who famously represented Norway and Finland, respectively, are Grieg and Sibelius. Composers who represented England include Elgar, Vaughan Williams, and Holst. Composers who represented Spain include Albéniz, Granados, and de Falla. Composers who represented Hungary include Bartók and Kodály. Nationalistic composers who represented the United States include Ives, Harris, Gershwin, and Copland.

NINETEENTH-CENTURY DEBATE OVER PROGRAM MUSIC AND ABSOLUTE MUSIC

In the 19th century, music philosophers debated the value of program music versus absolute music. **Programmatic music**, or music that represented non-musical images or ideas, flourished in the Romantic era with program symphonies, symphonic poems, and character pieces with descriptive titles. Examples of Romantic-period program music include *Don Quixote* by Richard Strauss, *Danse Macabre* by Camille Saint-Saëns, *Symphonie Fantastique* by Hector Berlioz, and *The Sorcerer's Apprentice* by Paul Dukas. **Absolute music** was defined by opponents of program music as instrumental music that existed apart from extra-musical references, able to move audiences solely on the purity of the music itself. Proponents of programmatic music argued that music alone could not express anything and that music needed associations for audiences to fully grasp musical expression. Recent scholars acknowledge that the divide over program music and absolute music is not as distinct as once believed, and is open to interpretation.

IMPACT OF VALVED HORNS AND TRUMPETS

Before the 19th century, horns had a range limited to the notes of the overtone series and to crooks or hand-stopping techniques that changed the pitch of the instrument. Although the hand-stopping technique added a wider range to the horn, tone and volume were highly variable. The trumpets of the Classical era were more limited than the horns; although they also had a range limited to the notes of the overtone series, hand-stopping techniques could not be used to add a wider range because of the length of the early trumpet. The invention of the **valved horn and keys** for the modern trumpet in 1814 allowed players to play chromatically throughout their entire range. Composers began to incorporate more brass into their orchestral writing and, as a result, brass instruments became essential instruments in any orchestra with leading parts and solos. The orchestral sound of the 19th century increased substantially in power and capacity, and composers such as Wagner, Strauss, Stravinsky, and Mahler became known for their tremendously large orchestrations and vast scope of sound.

Impressionist Movement

The Impressionist movement (~1890–1920 AD) in music was influenced by the synonymous movement in visual arts by painters such as Monet, Cézanne, Degas, Manet, and Renoir, in which subtle brushstrokes obscured any sharp lines to give a general "impression" of a scene without precise details. French composer Claude Debussy (1862–1918) developed a musical equivalent in which sound defied strict harmonic rules and soft instrumental colors focused on constant movement without distinct sectional borders, giving the audience a similar effect as in Impressionist art of a general experience rather than one that draws attention to specific details. Melodies tended to center around a single pitch without much climax, similar to the individual brushstrokes utilized by Impressionist painters of the time. Debussy was a key Impressionist composer; other composers who have worked in the Impressionist aesthetic include Maurice Ravel, Béla Bartók, Olivier Messiaen, György Ligeti, and George Crumb.

Schoenberg

Arnold Schoenberg (1874–1951) was an Austrian theorist and painter, and one of the most influential composers of his time. Schoenberg developed the **12-tone technique** of music in which all 12 pitches of the chromatic scale are treated as equal, rejecting the conventions of traditional tonality. The 12 pitches are ordered into a series that becomes the basic structure for the composition. The pitches can be in any range or duration, but they must be introduced in the composition in that order. Schoenberg's revolutionary system of composition broke away from the traditional tonality of the 20th century and abandoned any hint of a tonal center. The impact of Schoenberg's 12-tone system of composition continued in the music of Milton Babbitt, Pierre Boulez, Charles Wuorinen, Anton Webern, Karlheinz Stockhausen, Alban Berg, Luigi Nono, Roger Sessions, and multiple other composers.

Neoclassical Movement

At the end of the 19th century, Romantic music reached the height of expressive emotionalism with the large-scale works of program music by composers such as Tchaikovsky, Liszt, and Mahler. The beginning of the 20th century brought about **Modernism** and the rejection of tonality by experimental composers such as Schoenberg, Boulez, Berg, and Webern. **Neoclassicism** was a trend of the 20th century that emerged as a reaction to the emotionalism of the late Romantic era and the abandonment of tonality in the early-20th century. Composers of the neoclassical movement sought a return to the order, restraint, clarity, and formal balance of the music of the 18th century. Neoclassical music usually featured restraint, lighter texture, objectivity, a transparent melodic line, and a call to music of the past. Prominent composers of the neoclassical movement include Paul Hindemith, Igor Stravinsky, Richard Strauss, Sergei Prokofiev, Manuel de Falla, and Aaron Copland.

Minimalist Movement

Minimalism began as a compositional movement in the late 1960s, as a reaction to the traditional goal-oriented, narrative, and representational music of the previous centuries. As an extension of experimental music, **minimalist music** often features compositional techniques that emphasize the process of music rather than motion toward a goal. Minimalist composers sought to create music that uses a minimal amount of notes, minimal instruments, and minimal focal points, so that the music could become more a wall of sound than a goal-oriented mission. Minimalist music tends to have a consonant harmony, perpetually repeated patterns or drones, interlocking rhythmic phrases and rhythms, and gradual transformation. In minimalist music, the form tends to be continuous without well-defined separate sections; notes may be added to a repeating pattern slowly so that the resulting effect of the music becomes somewhat hypnotic. Representative minimalist composers include Steve Reich, Terry Riley, Philip Glass, John Adams, and La Monte Young.

Latin Jazz

Latin jazz is a style of jazz that originated in the late 1940s when musicians merged the rhythms and instruments of Afro-Latin music with American jazz music. The two prominent sub-genres of Latin jazz are Afro-Cuban jazz and Afro-Brazilian jazz. **Afro-Cuban jazz** incorporated Cuban rhythms such as the mambo and the habanera with elements of bebop. Afro-Cuban bass lines featured distinctive syncopated rhythms labeled as either a 2–3 clave or 3–2 clave. **Afro-Brazilian jazz** incorporated rhythms of the samba with music of Europe and America. A new style of samba known as bossa nova featured a laid-back singing style, increased textural complexity, and a distinctive rhythmic pattern known as the bossa nova clave. Famous Latin jazz musicians include Mario Bauzá, Luciano Pozo, Machito (Frank Grillo), W. C. Handy, Dizzy Gillespie, Antônio Carlos Jobim, and João Gilberto, among others.

Bossa Nova Movement

The bossa nova movement originated in Rio de Janeiro, Brazil, in the late 1950s and combined elements of the popular Brazilian samba with elements of American jazz. It soon became popular in the United States and then became an international sensation. **Bossa nova** is characterized by a laid-back singing style, complex harmonies, and a distinctive rhythmic pattern known as the **bossa nova clave**. The music of bossa nova often features acoustic guitar as a principal instrument and also includes bass, drums, voice, and piano. The bossa nova rhythm, often notated in duple meter, starts with a downbeat but is otherwise syncopated to give a swaying feeling rather than a strong, measured pulse. Central figures of the bossa nova movement include Antônio Carlos Jobim, João Gilberto, Vinícius de Moraes, Sérgio Mendes, Roberto Menescal, and Nara Leão. Famous tunes include "Chega de Saudade," "Girl from Ipanema," "Desafinado," "Corcovado," "Águas de Março," and "Mas Que Nada."

Blues

Music of the blues originated through African work songs that were brought over to the United States in the 19th and early-20th centuries. The rise of the **blues** occurred approximately around the time of the emancipation of slaves in the US, especially in the Mississippi delta and east Texas. Elements such as the call and response format, the unaccompanied voice, and accompaniment styles all have roots in traditional African music. By the mid-20th century, the blues had a standard 12-bar harmonic progression: I-I-I-I-IV-IV-I-I-V-IV-I-I. The blues also utilizes the **blues scale** that features a lowered third and a dominant seventh, called the "blue notes." Music usually centers on a melancholy emotion, with instrumental and vocal techniques such as moans, growls, and cries to express that emotion. Famous blues musicians include Blind Lemon Jefferson, Charley Patton, Blind Blake, Blind Willie McTell, Lead Belly, Bukka White, Big Bill Broonzy, Muddy Waters, B. B. King, and T-Bone Walker.

Leitmotif

The term leitmotif is used to identify a reoccurring motivic fragment that musically represents some part of a musical drama, usually a person, place, or idea. The **leitmotif** must be clearly recognizable by its melody, harmonic progression, or rhythm. In the context of an opera, the leitmotif becomes a useful tool for composers as a means of character development and the unfolding of the story. In a musical drama, the leitmotif can reinforce the action taking place onstage, as well as recall an event or person from a previous scene. The leitmotif can also be modified through **thematic transformation** and even combined with other leitmotifs to suggest a change in the narrative and the characters' relationships. The term is most often associated with Wagner's later operatic works, although he preferred the terms *Grundthema* and *Hauptmotiv* instead.

Evolution of Harmonic Language

Harmonic language before Wagner (1813–1883) was dominated by the rules of diatonicism and straightforward voice leading. By the middle of the 19th century, composers started to explore ideas of chromaticism and common tone relationships rather than strong root progressions. The arrival of Wagner's *Tristan und Isolde* in 1865 brought a major change to the harmonic language of the past and signaled a new era of modern compositional techniques. In the four-hour opera, chromaticism plays a prominent role in the dissolution of typical harmonic expectation. Now known as the **Tristan chord**, the leitmotif of the main character reveals a functionally ambiguous tritone chord (f-b-d#'-g#'), which, instead of resolving, progresses to another equally chromatic and dissonant tritone chord. Wagner's use of harmonic suspension, full chromaticism, polyphony, and range of colors in *Tristan und Isolde* paved the way to the modern collapse of traditional tonal writing and to the advent of experimental, atonal compositions of the 20th century such as those of Bruckner, Mahler, and Schoenberg.

Organum

Organum is considered to be one of the earliest forms of polyphony and appeared in the Medieval period in the 9th century. **Organum** was based on a cantus firmus and began as improvised voices that duplicated the original melody. Organum types included parallel voices at the octave and parallel voices at the fifth below. Composers adjusted the lines to avoid tritones as necessary. Organum expanded to include contrary and oblique motion, as well as free or florid organum in which the tenor chant held notes and upper voices decorated the tenor with phrases of varying length. In the 12th century, the development of the **discant** in organum moved the compositional techniques further toward polyphony as voices became increasingly complex and independent. By the 13th century, the motet had replaced organum as a major polyphonic genre.

Classic Greek Tragedy

Ancient Greek tragedies hold an important influence on the modern opera and theatre of today. Many of the initial developments of modern opera and theatre were based on this classic form that arose in the 6th century BC. The elements of a classic tragedy include plot, character, thought, diction, melody, and spectacle. In a classic Greek tragedy, the hero often has a goal but encounters limits through human frailty, the gods, or nature, and usually encounters suffering. The characters of a tragedy must show **essential qualities** or morals that remain consistent throughout the plot. **Thought** is often displayed through a Greek tragedy to drive the plot line and to reveal key plot elements. **Diction** must be clear and serve the lines of the tragedy as one of the most important elements of tragedy. **Melody** is subservient to words and should only be used to accessorize the plot. **Spectacle** refers to the setting of the drama and, like melody, should be used as an accessory.

Opera Seria vs. Opera Buffa

By the end of the 17th century, opera as a musical form had been widely accepted. Two genres appeared as the philosophical focus as the new century turned its attention to the Enlightenment. Thinkers and composers of the Enlightenment held that opera should reflect ancient Greek values such as clarity and unity, structure, and propriety; the **opera seria** that arose during this time focused on tragic and serious subjects that were historical rather than mythical. The structure, number of singers, and plot line were organized so that the action usually took place in three acts with alternating arias and recitatives, and the number of characters usually numbered six or seven, with two to four main characters. **Opera buffa**, in contrast, focused on humorous and light-hearted elements. There was often a wide range of characters, and spoken dialogue replaced recitative. The form was less structured and often featured prominent orchestral and instrumental parts. Music tended to be faster and helped portray comic elements of the plot line, such as laughter and sneezing.

Authentic Musical Modes

The authentic musical modes are commonly used in modern times and have origins in the Medieval musical tradition as well as the Greek musical tradition. The most commonly known authentic musical modes are Ionian, Dorian, Phrygian, Lydian, Mixolydian, Aeolian, and Locrian. The **Ionian** mode is also known as the major scale in modern musical theory. **Dorian** is similar to the natural minor scale, but has a raised sixth scale degree. **Phrygian** is similar to the natural minor scale, but has a lowered second scale degree. **Lydian** is similar to the major scale, but has a raised fourth scale degree. **Mixolydian** is similar to the major scale, but has a lowered seventh scale degree. **Aeolian** is also known as the natural minor scale in modern musical theory. **Locrian** is similar to the natural minor scale, but has a lowered second scale degree and a lowered fifth scale degree.

Classical Sonata Form

The sonata form has been a key compositional structure since the Classical era in the mid- to late-18th century. Usually referring to a convention within a single movement of a sonata or symphony, the **sonata form** features three main sections: the exposition, development, and recapitulation. The melodic and harmonic themes of the movement are usually introduced in the **exposition**. The initial first subject is introduced in the tonic key, while the second subject is usually in the dominant or relative minor key. In a typical sonata form, a bridge or a short transition connects the first and second subjects. In the **development** section, the thematic material from the exposition is altered, modified, and transformed through mood, key, and modulations. The development section of a sonata form introduces tension that demands resolution; tension builds until the beginning of the **recapitulation**, in which tonal balance is reinstated with a shortened version of the initial subject and the second subject, this time in the tonic key instead of the dominant or relative minor. A coda may round out the sonata at the end.

Classical Symphonic Form

The symphony was a major compositional form in the Classical era (~1750–1820 AD) and refers to a large musical work usually for orchestra or another combination of instruments in four movements. The **classical symphonic form** has a fast first movement, a slow second movement, a dance form in the third movement, and a fast fourth movement. The first movement is usually in sonata allegro form, which contains an exposition, development, and recapitulation. The second slow movement is usually in a gentle, lyrical ABA pattern or a theme and variations. The third movement is typically in a dance form such as the Minuet and Trio or the Scherzo. The fourth movement is typically in Rondo form, or Sonata Rondo form, in which a principal theme in the tonic key alternates with new episodes: ABACADA...etc.

Operas vs. Oratorios

Opera began as an art form in the late-16th century and consisted of a staged dramatic work with singers and orchestra. **Oratorios** began as an art form in the 17th century and became popular in part because of the success of opera and because of religious bans on secular operas during Lent. Both opera and oratorio are large-scale musical works that feature dramatic, musical, and narrative elements. The two forms both utilize solo vocalists, chorus, ensembles, and orchestras. However, opera is usually theatrically staged, while oratorio is not. Also, oratorio usually centers on a religious or ethical subject, while opera usually centers on historical, mythological, or other secular plot lines. Famous operas include Jacopo Peri's *Dafne*, Gioachino Rossini's *Barber of Seville*, Giacomo Puccini's *Madame Butterfly*, W.A. Mozart's *The Marriage of Figaro*, Giuseppe Verdi's *La Traviata*, and Georges Bizet's *Carmen*. Famous oratorios include G.F. Handel's *Messiah*, Joseph Haydn's *Creation*, and Felix Mendelssohn's *Elijah*.

Waltz Form

The waltz is a dance form that has been popular since the late-18th century and features triple meter in a lively tempo. The term literally means "to turn about," and musical aspects of the **waltz** help dancers feel the refined and fluid motion of the turn. In waltz time, emphasis is on the downbeat, while the other two beats create a sense of floating, as on the dance floor. Early forms of the waltz featured two simple repeated phrases of about eight measures. As the dance evolved, the waltz became longer in form and more complex, with introductory material as well as a coda. The ballroom dance achieved popularity across all of Europe and reached its height of fashion with the **Viennese waltz**. Representative composers of the Viennese waltz include Joseph Lanner, Johann Strauss, Franz Schubert, Frédéric Chopin, Franz Liszt, Johannes Brahms, and Pyotr Tchaikovsky.

Changes Giving Rise to the Renaissance Movement

The period of 1400–1600 AD was a time of major change not only in Western musical history, but also in Western history in general. The 1400s marked the end of the Hundred Years' War, the fall of the Byzantine Empire, and the end of the Great Schism. During the **Renaissance**, religious conflicts emerged through the Reformation, European colonialism expanded, and a middle class grew in many European nations. As a result of the Ottoman Turks' victory in 1453, displaced Byzantine scholars brought ancient Greek writings with them to other European countries, and the Western world had access to the plays and histories of ancient Greece for the first time. Renaissance art featured classical Greek and Roman ideals of humanism, clarity, and clean form. As a result, music of the Renaissance featured Greek modes, clarity of vocal lines, harmonic consonance, imitative counterpoint, and expressivity. The **printing press** was also invented during this time around 1440, so music became widely available to the expanding middle class.

Baroque Music

Music of the Baroque era (~1600–1750 AD), was influenced by the rise of rationalism in the philosophy of the time. Composers sought to portray emotions through objectivity rather than subjectivity, and the expression of any one piece or movement was limited to a single affect. Thoroughbass was prominent during the Baroque era, and a Baroque ensemble would typically read music and improvise on the figured bass, also known as continuo. **Ornamentation** was used heavily in the Baroque period and consisted of embellished notes of a musical line. These included trills, mordents, and grace notes that were rarely written out but instead were improvised by the performers. Famous composers of the Baroque era include Claudio Monteverdi, Girolamo Frescobaldi, Arcangelo Corelli, Antonio Vivaldi, Domenico Scarlatti, François Couperin, Jean-Philippe Rameau, Georg Philipp Telemann, G.F. Handel, J.S. Bach, and Henry Purcell.

Influence of African Song and Dance on Latin American Music

The historically large African population found in the Caribbean region near South America has had a substantial influence on the development of Latin American music. Common features of African music include call and response singing, repeated and improvised musical figures, polyrhythm, and the use of African instruments such as congas, rattles, thumb pianos, claves, and drum ensembles. **Calypso** music, originally developed in Trinidad in the early 19th century, is a popular song and dance form in the Caribbean. Typically played with a steel drum band, calypso music is witty, lively, and humorous. The **rumba**, originating in the late 19th century, is another African song and dance form now popular in Cuba that uses conga drums and sticks. The rumba has a three-part form with fast polyrhythms, and includes improvised verses and repetitive call and response sections. The **merengue**, becoming prominent in both the Dominican Republic and Haiti in the middle of the 19th century, is a popular song and dance style in a swift duple meter. Instruments with some African influences include the double-headed tambora drum and the metal guayo scraper.

Pre-Columbian Indigenous Musical Culture of South America

Most of the Pre-Columbian indigenous musical culture of South America studied today is drawn from the Inca of Peru and the Aztecs of central Mexico. The Spanish conquerors of the 16th century recorded the role of music in these highly developed civilizations. The Inca and Aztecs produced public ceremonies, professional musicians, and musician-specific educational institutions. Aztec and Inca rulers employed musicians who were responsible for new compositions and performances of large repertoires. Standards of performance were held high, and a mistake in a ceremonial performance or dance could mean death. Since no evidence has been found of a Pre-Columbian musical notation, little is known about the actual sound and style of their music. However, evidence from Aztec and Inca sites reveals instruments such as the huehuetl and teponaztli types of drums, gourd rattles, flutes and panpipes, clay jingles, wood and conch shell trumpets, bone rasps, and ocarinas.

Mambo

The mambo is a song and dance genre of music that stems from the Afro-Cuban movement of the 1940s. The form developed in Cuba with influences from Mexico and the USA, as well as those from European dances and African rhythms. The genre soon became popular in Latin America and crossed over to the United States, where the mambo dance became a ballroom staple, especially in New York City. **Mambo** is performed by an ensemble that usually consists of double bass, bongo, tumbadora, trumpets, guitar, and voices. The mambo rhythms are moderate to fast and feature distinctive riffs for the rhythm section and brass instruments. Cowbells often play strong syncopations over the second beat in a mambo ostinato, while the conga drum varies struck tones through unaccented strokes, strongly accented strokes, and open tones.

Early Broadway Songwriters and American Musical Theater

The first Broadway songwriters of the 1920s included Irving Berlin, Jerome Kern, the Gershwins, Harold Arlen, Oscar Hammerstein, Richard Rodgers, and Cole Porter. American musical theater of the early 20th century was intricately tied to the New York music industry called **Tin Pan Alley**, a geographical location where musicians and composers came together to create popular new songs for the working class as a reaction against upper-class parlor music. The style borrowed heavily from the jazz scene as well as African-American sounds and themes. The success of Tin Pan Alley songs depended on large-scale production and stage shows on Broadway, and the first Broadway shows were loosely related singing, dancing, and vaudeville music from Tin Pan Alley. Historians mark ***Show Boat*** (1927) by Kern and Hammerstein as the first full-fledged Broadway musical with a complete beginning-to-end plot.

Review Video: Musicals vs Plays
Visit mometrix.com/academy and enter code: 537548

Appalachian Music

Appalachian music refers to the folk traditions of the Eastern US, specifically the Appalachian mountain range. The music is heavily influenced by the Irish, Scottish, and English emigrants of the 18th century and features musical traditions such as English and Scottish ballads, dance tunes, and fiddle songs. African-American musical traditions also contributed to the development of **Appalachian music**, and conventional aspects of the genre, such as the banjo, strong rhythmic drive, harmonic blue notes, and group singing, all originate from African-American slaves of the time. Appalachian music features heavy ornamentation, improvisation, rhythmic and melodic focus, and an upbeat tempo. Typical instruments used in the genre include the banjo, mandolin, guitar, autoharp, American fiddle, fretted dulcimer, dobro, and dulcimer.

Early Jazz Music

Early jazz music originated from a wide variety of cultural, social, and instrumental influences from the 1890s through the 1910s. **New Orleans jazz** was one of the earliest forms of jazz music and borrowed from the music of black and creole musicians; it featured frequent interplay between instruments, improvisations, and syncopated march rhythms. Early jazz music, as well as blues music, was heavily influenced by the black church through improvisation, storytelling, call and response, vocal inflections, and the blues progression. Early jazz music also borrowed features of American marching band music and ragtime, such as strong stride rhythms and multi-thematic material. Pianistic harmonies of composers such as Debussy and Ravel also contributed to early jazz music, and jazz composers also incorporated the claves and syncopations of Latin song and dance forms.

Waltz vs. Mazurka

Both the waltz and the mazurka were important European dances of the Romantic era and became popular compositional forms in the 1800s. The waltz originated in southern Germany and Austria in the 13th century, while the **mazurka** originated in the province of Mazovia in Poland in the 16th century. Both dances feature triple time; however, the waltz places emphasis on the downbeat while the mazurka places emphasis on either the second or third beats. Both dances usually consisted of two or four repeated eight-measure sections; however, the waltz eventually evolved to become a longer complex work within art music and included an introduction as well as a coda. The waltz usually held a faster tempo with an elegant style, but stylistic variation among mazurkas was common. **Obertas** were livelier and more jovial versions; **kujawiak** were slower and more melancholic forms of the mazurka, while the conventional mazurka typically featured an intense, militant aesthetic.

Importance of Arab Culture in the Development of North African Music

The region of North Africa received considerable cultural influence from the bordering Arabic countries, and the music of North Africa reflects that cultural diversity. The North African region that includes present-day Morocco, Libya, Tunisia, and Algeria is also known by the Arabic term **Maghreb** ("west"). Although Egypt is geographically included on the African continent, it holds its own unique cultural, musical, and sociopolitical place within North Africa. Arabic-Islamists ruled the Maghreb from approximately the 7th century to the 16th century. Beginning in the eleventh century, Jewish and Muslim refugees from the al-Andalus region of the Iberian Peninsula brought with them the Arab-Andalusian music traditions that originated in Baghdad. Elements of Arabic influence in North African music include the Quranic chant, poetry/harp/lute playing, and instruments such as the gimbri, drums, and metal castanets.

West African Musical Traditions

West Africa holds several local musical traditions such as those used in praise singing, various ceremonies, work activities, and national identities. Historically, court musicians were responsible for continuing the **oral tradition** through singing and performing several instruments such as the lute, long trumpet, fiddle, and drum. Drum ensembles in south Ghana frequently use bell patterns, but those in Senegal, Niger, and other parts of Ghana use the talking drum, one of the oldest instruments in West Africa, dating back to the 7th century. Music plays an important role in birth, adulthood initiations, marriages, and death through singing, drumming, and dancing. During ceremonies, professional musicians perform special music to induce trance, possession, or direct communication with spirits. **Praise singing** emerged in the 20th century through the Ghanaian musical genre called highlife, which incorporates guitar playing with traditional Akan music.

Djembe

The djembe is a rope-tuned, skin-covered drum dating back to the Mali Empire around 1230 AD that can produce a variety of pitches through different hand-striking techniques and drum positions. Typically made of hollowed-out wood, the **djembe** yields a large sound relative to its size and has been used for speech-like communication. Up until the 1950s, the djembe was only known in its local West African ethnic groups, but it has since become popular in Western culture as well. In a traditional African ensemble, multiple drums are used, including a lead djembe and other dunun. Drummers repeat various rhythmic figures, resulting in polyrhythms, while the lead djembe accentuates dancers' movements and improvises over the rest of the drumming ensemble. Musicians and singers typically form a circle with the dancers on the inside.

Use of Dialogue in African Musical Form and Rhythm

Dialogue, also known as call and response, is an important and unique feature of African musical expression. Within musical aesthetics, **dialogue** occurs when a musical line "responds" to a previous musical line; this response can come from a different musician, instrument, group, or register within a solo performer. A vocal or instrumental leader might make a call, and another musician or group of musicians might respond with a musical interjection so that phrases are exchanged between the two groups. Solo performers can also have a musical dialogue through musical or extra-musical interjections such as whistles, percussive sounds, or other alternating musical phrases. The call and response form has been an influential African musical element that can be seen in the genres of blues, jazz, hip-hop, rock, and gospel.

Traditional African Music

Although the continent of Africa holds a great variety of musical expressions, traditions, and instruments among its different regions, certain musical elements remain uniquely African. The **call and response form** that has so heavily influenced other modern musical genres has been a central feature of African music for centuries. Also distinctive is the use of polyrhythms, syncopation, and offbeat phrasing in rhythmic patterns of the area. Much of African music uses a **cyclic form** in which various phrases with a set number of beats can be continued as long as the performers want; musicians can begin at any part of the cycle and frequently improvise over the form. Instruments that jingle, buzz, or rattle are also popular in African cultures; examples include the mbira, the dagbamba, and xylophones, lutes, and harps that have been manipulated to buzz, jingle, or rattle when played.

Kabuki

Kabuki is a Japanese theater form stemming from the Edo period of the 1600s that was originally performed by females, but is now performed by males as well. Kesho, the kabuki makeup, is a hallmark of the art form in which a white Oshiroi base is decorated with boldly colored kumadori to produce exaggerated and dramatic masks. There are three types of kabuki: **jidaimono** are historical plays; **sewamono** are domestic theater dramas; and **shosagoto** are dance pieces. The form of a kabuki play generally contains four parts: the first part called the deha includes two sections that introduce the mood and the characters (oki and michiyuki). The second part called the chuha includes two sections that build the plot emotionally and climactically (kudoki and monogatari). The third part called the odoriji is a dance component. The fourth part called the iriha includes both the musical finale and the end of the plot (chirashi and dangire).

Middle Eastern Maqam System of Melodic Organization

The maqam system of melodic organization used in Middle Eastern music most resembles the Western mode but is distinctively confined to the lower tetrachord. There are more than 30 different maqamat, and each defines the melodic contour, pitches, and hierarchical development of the scale. The Middle Eastern maqam, which came into use in the 9th century, is not even-tempered as in Western music, as fifth notes are tuned based on the third harmonic; additionally, each of the remaining notes may be tuned differently depending on which maqam is being used. Scalar intervals may include approximations of quartertones, semitones, and even microtones. Musicians frequently compose and improvise over a single maqam but may also modulate to others before returning. Since the nature of the Middle Eastern maqam contains numerous subtle microtonal variations, music of the region is mostly melodic and is rarely ever harmonic.

Traditional Chinese Musical Instruments

The **pipa** is a pear-shaped Chinese plucked lute traditionally made with silk thread that has four strings and a bent neck. The pipa has been an important and popular instrument of Chinese culture since the 7th century and is often played as a solo instrument in performance. The standard tuning for the pipa, A-d-c-a, allows the full chromatic scale to be played. The **erhu** is another traditional Chinese lute often featured as a solo instrument and has two strings with a bow that sits in between the strings. The traditional instrument is typically made with snakeskin on the sound box and horsehair for the bow. The **yangqin** is a trapezoidal, hammered dulcimer that is often played solo as well as in ensembles. The **dizi** is a transverse flute that plays an important role in Chinese folk, operatic, and orchestral music. The instrument includes a special hole in addition to the blowing and finger holes that, when applied, gives the resulting sounds a nasal and buzzing quality.

Australian Aboriginal Music

Australian Aboriginal Musical Instruments

Australian Aboriginal musical instruments include the didgeridoo, the bull-roarer, and the gum leaf. The **didgeridoo**, most well-known of the Aboriginal instruments, has been used for at least 1500 years and consists of a simple wooden tube that is slightly flared at the end. Didgeridoo musicians buzz their lips similarly to trumpet players but without a mouthpiece. The sound produced by the didgeridoo is likened to a low-pitched drone and is often used to accompany songs or traditional stories. The **bull-roarer** consists of a simple wooden slat connected to the end of a length of cord. Sound is produced when the cord is wound and the bull-roarer is whirled in a circular motion. The aerodynamics of this instrument creates a pulsing, low-pitched roar. The **gum leaf** is a more primitive Aboriginal instrument, yet still plays an important role in the culture and tradition of native Australians. Musicians use the leaf of the Eucalyptus tree, held taut against the lip, as a simple wind valve for the mouth. Skilled players can easily play tunes using the same techniques as in whistling.

Role of Music in Australian Aboriginal Culture

Music played a key role in Australian Aboriginal culture through storytelling, preserving history, and leading ceremonies. Since there was no formal system of writing, the Aborigines held a strong **oral tradition**; records were passed down through generations via song and dance. The Aborigines believed that all music comes from the spiritual realm, and new songs were discovered through visions and dreams. Music played an integral role in Aboriginal daily life, and children were encouraged at an early age to sing and dance while doing everyday tasks. The Aborigines had songs that recorded family histories, geographies of the land, rules, and customs. The Aborigines also had secular gossip songs about controversies and relationships. Ceremonial music played an important role in the various spiritual ceremonies, whether to invoke ancestral beings or to purify items of the deceased.

Polynesian Nose Flute

The **nose flute** is a widely important wind instrument throughout the Pacific, except for Australia and New Zealand. Commonly made out of bamboo, the nose flute is played through a single nostril, while the other nostril is held shut. Since the nose flute produces a soft and gentle sound, it played an important role in many Polynesian musical traditions. The nose flute was popular during courtship and lovemaking; the timbre and tone of the nose flute had an enticing sound, and as a quiet instrument, encouraged intimacy and privacy for current and prospective lovers. In Tonga, the nose flute was also used as a respectful way to gently awaken the chief of a tribe. Some cultures believed that nose flutes were also instruments that could evoke magical and spiritual qualities.

Contributions of Women to Music Composition

While most of the historical record is made up of male composers, women have always had a place in composition throughout history. Below is a brief record of female composers throughout the ages.

- **Hildegard von Bingen (1098–1179)** – 12th century German abbess, composer, and writer.
- **Fanny Mendelssohn (1805–1847)** – Early 19th century composer, writing many of her works under the name of her brother, Felix Mendelssohn.
- **Clara Schumann (1819–1896)** – 19th century composer and pianist, known for influencing Romantic music with her piano compositions.
- **Amy Beach (1867–1944)** – Late 19th and early 20th century composer.
- **Lili Boulanger (1893–1918)** – Early 20th century French composer known for choral and orchestral works. She was the first female to win the Prix de Rome, a major scholarship by the French government, enabling artists to travel to Rome to study.
- **Florence Price (1887–1953)** – Early to mid-20th century African-American composer. She was the first black woman to have her work performed by a major US orchestra (Chicago Symphony Orchestra, 1933).
- **Ma Rainey (1886–1939)** – Early 20th century blues singer.
- **Bessie Smith (1894–1937)** – Blues singer primarily active in the 1920s and 1930s.
- **Sister Rosetta Tharpe (1915–1973)** – Gospel and blues musician in the 1930s to the 1960s. Her work went on to heavily influence developing rock and roll music.
- **Astrud Gilberto (1940–2023)** – Brazilian Bossa Nova singer and songwriter popular in the 1960s.

Music Instruction and Assessment

Effects of Physical, Cognitive, and Social Development on Music Learning

As students progress through puberty in ages 10–14 for girls and 12–16 for boys, there are many changes physically, cognitively, and socially that affect their music learning. Students will be going through growth spurts, and their reference for posture or instrument positioning may need to be adjusted accordingly. Also, **voice development** will affect vocal students as the larynx enlarges and the vocal cords lengthen and thicken. The physiological changes of the vocal mechanisms tend to affect boys more than girls, evident in the "cracking" of the voice. During puberty, students will have to work toward singing voice production, pitch accuracy, increasing vocal range, and maintaining a positive attitude toward choral singing. Cognitively, students in puberty are increasingly able to process conceptual ideas and should work on self-regulating musical activities and performances. Socially, students in puberty tend to need more opportunities for self-expression, autonomy, and acceptance in their music learning.

Principles of Sequencing a Music Curriculum

Principles of sequencing a music curriculum can be based on three different techniques: content sequencing, task sequencing, or sequencing of elaboration. When **sequencing based on content**, the instructor should analyze the content for the main item and then organize the general content into a hierarchal structure. The most general and inclusive content should be presented first, leading the way to more detailed ideas while all the while relating them to former learning content. When **sequencing based on a task**, the instructor should analyze the skill involved and order the learning progression from simple, more elementary tasks toward more complex skills that build on previous tasks. When **sequencing based on elaboration**, the students are given an overall view of the knowledge, then they are presented with basic content before progressing toward more detailed information while keeping the organizing, overarching theme in place.

Use of the Socratic Method

The Socratic method refers to the philosophy of education as set by the ancient Greek philosopher **Socrates**, which advocates the use of questions in developing a student's critical thinking and intellect. Rather than lecturing or simply telling the student educational content, the questions compel the student to use critical thinking for a solution or answer. The music educator can utilize this philosophy of education in all areas of music education, and especially in guided listening to teach students self-assessment, critical thinking, and how to develop one's own musical expression. Music educators can ask guided questions such as "How do the expressive elements of this performance inform your own playing?" to foster a sense of self-assessment in the student's music listening. Asking **open-ended** questions rather than yes/no questions will further develop the student's critical thinking abilities and intellectual curiosity, translating the analysis of guided listening to his or her own musical practice and growth.

Teaching Musical Aesthetics and Expression

Music educators can use various techniques to teach musical aesthetics and expression in their students. Instructors should use the technique of **modeling** often, to demonstrate various physical and aural attributes of an expression to the student. The student should have various visual and aural models of expressive representation to help integrate the technique and sound into his or her own expressive voice. The music educator can also use **guided listening** to teach musical aesthetics to students. As another method of modeling, the student will be able to listen to the individual expression of other performers in developing a personal musical aesthetic. The music educator can also analyze, reflect, and evaluate musical performances together with the students, so that the students will be able to think critically and creatively in analyzing, reflecting, and evaluating their own unique musical aesthetic and expression.

Incorporating Music Theory Instruction During a Full Rehearsal

As a music educator, it is important to incorporate music theory instruction during full rehearsals, ensuring that a student's musical education is a comprehensive, all-encompassing one, and not one solely focused on performance. A thorough musical education will allow the student an informed and deeper understanding of music. When possible, the music educator should introduce new **theoretical concepts** before rehearsing a piece; the instructor should not take too much time in explanation, but give only concise, direct introduction, as the immersion within the music will aid in a student's understanding. When the music educator interrupts the rehearsal to do spot checks, the instructor should use appropriate language in explaining the technical or musical problem, to further integrate the concept of music theory into musical performance and understanding. When time allows, the music educator can give brief verbal quizzes, to keep the students accountable for their musical theory learning.

Practical Teaching Techniques

Accommodating Aural Learners

Students whose primary learning style is that of aural learning need specific teaching techniques to help them succeed. **Aural learners** learn best by hearing educational content, so teachers should frequently use precise terms when explaining an idea. Aural learners also learn through talking and discussion, so a useful teaching technique is allowing students to discuss ideas and content among themselves. Aural learners may need to question and talk through ideas to help fully comprehend educational content, so teachers should not brush off students' questions, but allow ample time for student questions and answers. Another technique to accommodate aural learners is to have spoken quizzes and tests, to allow aural learners the opportunity to talk through a concept. A helpful technique particularly for aural music learners is to listen to a **recording** of one's own rehearsals to be able to listen for mistakes and areas for improvement.

Accommodating Visual Learners

Students whose primary learning style is that of visual learning need specific teaching techniques to help them succeed. **Visual learners** learn best by seeing educational content. When teachers are explaining educational content or instructions, they should also provide a visual explanation, either through a projector or handouts, or by demonstrating the concepts visually. Educators can also encourage visual learners to make **flashcards**, a helpful tool to visually learn content. Other practical tools for visual learners are pictures, diagrams, and concept maps. These all allow students to visually integrate the learning content. When demonstrating instrumental technique or posture, the educator should make sure that all students can see; without a visual model, visual learners will have a harder time assimilating the new concepts and skills.

Accommodating Kinesthetic Learners

Students whose primary learning style is that of kinesthetic learning need specific teaching techniques to help them succeed. **Kinesthetic learners** learn best by doing, and need to integrate movement with the introduction of new educational concepts and ideas. Music educators should implement teaching techniques that require students to move while learning new educational content. Lesson segments should be kept short with frequent breaks to stand up and move. When introducing concepts such as rhythm and meter, the music educator should require students to **physically move** to the various rhythms and meters to accommodate those who are kinesthetic learners. When teaching specific instrumental techniques, the instructor should make sure that the kinesthetic learner demonstrates the movement or technique, rather than merely verbally or visually explaining the concept. Educators can also implement frequent games, field trips, and seating changes if appropriate.

Accommodations in the Music Classroom

Accommodating Students with Physical Disabilities

When a music classroom is able to accommodate students with physical disabilities, there are numerous benefits for both the students with disabilities as well as the average student. **Inclusion** promotes social awareness and acceptance, increased motor development, and higher mental acuity. Music educators can accommodate students with physical disabilities in a number of ways. The music classroom should be **ADA-accessible** and free from obstacles or other hazards. Also, the instructor can acquire **adaptive instruments** that allow students with physical disabilities the opportunity to develop motor and aural skills on a real instrument. Instructionally, educators should be sure to include lessons that require minimal physical strength; this inclusive teaching strategy will encourage confidence and self-esteem for students with physical disabilities. Educational goals should be appropriately sequenced to facilitate outcomes that are realistic and achievable.

Accommodating Students with Visual Impairments

Since the student with visual impairment will not have the visual aspect to aid their learning, music educators should focus on other modalities of learning (i.e., aural and tactile methods) to help the visually impaired student succeed. If the student with **visual impairment** is learning how to play an instrument, the educator should allow ample time for the student to physically explore the instrument and take it apart if possible. The student should also have the chance to explore other examples of the instrument so the student can fully conceptualize the instrument's shape and various other aspects. The music instructor should use the **Braille Music Code** for lessons on staff notation; students should not be expected to rely solely on their aural awareness of music, but should be able to learn musical notation as well. When demonstrating instrumental technique and movement, the educator should demonstrate the action by placing his or her hand under the student's hand.

Helping Students with Dyslexia Understand Written Musical Notation

Students with dyslexia tend to have difficulty with visual tracking, visual stress, visual-motor comprehension, sound discrimination, and symbol-sound relationships. Without the proper guidance from the music educators, the student with **dyslexia** may feel alienated from the educational curriculum, as well as from peers and the overall learning process. The music educator should begin by removing any barriers to the student's learning and helping to build on the student's strengths. Musical notation can be **enlarged** so that visual processing for the student will be easier. The student can also use **color-coded overlays** to prevent visual stress from an all-white background as well as to highlight certain aspects of the score. The music educator should also use a **multi-sensory approach** to teaching musical notation, including Dalcroze and Kodály techniques, visual and aural demonstrations of rhythm, visual and tactile demonstrations of notation, accessible technology, pattern learning, and graphics within the notation.

Review Video: Disorders that Impair Reading and Writing
Visit mometrix.com/academy and enter code: 306758

Sample Semester Assessment Plan

Music educators should use assessment strategies that include both individual student achievement as well as group ensemble achievement. A **comprehensive rubric** provides accountability for each student's musical growth within an ensemble setting. A **sample semester assessment plan** should include individual grading criteria such as performance of technical scales and musical excerpts, correct pitch matching, and correct rhythm matching. Students should be able to demonstrate historical and contextual knowledge of the appropriate music, and should demonstrate thoughtful analysis and evaluation of music. **Group grading criteria** can include attendance at performances, attendance at local concerts, chamber music participation, and solo/ensemble festival participation. **Classroom criteria** can include rehearsal preparation and readiness. The weight of each section could be graded as follows: individual performance: 30 percent; ensemble performance: 30 percent; classroom participation: 30 percent; other: 10 percent.

TEACHER FEEDBACK

Assessments in the music classroom can be a time-consuming activity; thus, it is highly useful and efficient to integrate as many informal assessment techniques as possible throughout the music rehearsal. **Informal assessments** can take the form of teacher feedback, short on-the-spot quizzes, and informal questioning and discussion. Not only will these informal assessments keep the students accountable for their daily musical progress, they will also give the music educator a formative assessment of the students' progress. When giving **short on-the-spot performance tests**, the teacher has the opportunity to gauge the progress of the individual or section; the educator can provide quick, succinct feedback on accuracy, technique, or any other issues that arise. **Informal questioning and discussion** relating to the analysis of the music also allows the teacher to assess and provide appropriate feedback to help the students' comprehension of the matter. The more feedback the teacher can provide, the more learning opportunities will be available for the students.

Review Video: Formative and Summative Assessments
Visit mometrix.com/academy and enter code: 804991

MUSIC PERFORMANCE OUTCOMES DICTATING ASSESSMENT COMPONENTS

The National Association for Music Education has published Performance Standards of musical outcomes and student abilities by grade level. These **Performance Standards** should provide a guideline for the music educator for assessment criteria. Students should be able to sing alone and with others, and they should demonstrate correct technical and musical ability and in a wide range of styles. Similarly, students should be able to play an instrument alone and with others while demonstrating correct technical and musical ability in a wide range of styles. Students should be able to improvise basic melodies and basic accompaniments on their instrument or through singing. Students should be able to compose and arrange music within specific contexts, both with or without technology. Students should be able to read and notate music appropriate to their level. Students should be able to listen to music and then analyze or describe it. Students should be able to evaluate music and musical performances. Students should also be able to relate music to non-musical fields such as history, visual art, and literature.

Relationship between Music and Other Disciplines

Impressionism in the Visual Arts vs. Impressionism in the Musical Arts

Impressionism began as a visual arts movement at the end of the 19th century and beginning of the 20th century with the works of Édouard Manet, Claude Monet, Edgar Degas, Pierre-Auguste Renoir, Berthe Morisot, Camille Pissarro, Alfred Sisley, and Mary Cassatt. The painters of the **Impressionist movement** sought to move away from the highly defined traditional paintings of the official salons of the day, and to create works that caught the brief, sensory effect of a particular moment through optical effects of light, color, and atmosphere. The painters used soft brushstrokes, abandoning any sharp lines to evoke a sense of haze and smoke in their work. The Impressionist movement in the visual arts paralleled the musical movement of the 19th and 20th centuries as well. In the music of Claude Debussy, formal elements such as distinct tonalities, cadences, and line were abandoned, while soft effects such as non-climactic melodies, complex textures, misty instrumental colors, and continuously changing forms all contributed to fleeting moments of musical color.

Literary and Musical Background of the Ballade Genre

The ballade refers to a literary and musical form in which words are set to three stanzas with seven or eight lines each. The original literary form of the **ballade** usually featured a narrative that could be comic, romantic, tragic, or historical. Although ballades have been around since Medieval times, renewed interest in the Romantic era helped the genre to flourish in the 18th and 19th centuries. Poets who often wrote ballades that were then set to music include Goethe, Schiller, Fontane, Heine, Platen, and Chamisso. Notable ballade composers who set literary ballades to music include Schubert, Schumann, Liszt, Wagner, and Strauss. By the middle of the nineteenth century, composers started to write purely **instrumental ballades**; Chopin wrote four piano ballades, most likely based on poems by Mickiewicz, and both Liszt and Brahms wrote instrumental piano ballades.

Integrating Music Instruction with Common Core Subjects

Music educators have the unique opportunity of integrating subjects outside of the fine arts with musical instruction. While focusing on musical instruction, the students can be fully immersed in broader musical learning as well as language arts, history, math, and science. When discussing musical phrasing, music educators can relate questions and answers in music to questions and answers in English. The students can also examine how individual phrases within music reinforce the work as a whole, the same way an individual sentence or paragraph relates to a written text as a whole. Teachers can use repertoire selections to reinforce historical knowledge as well, whether it be the Industrial Revolution during the Romantic era, or the Greek and Roman revival of the Renaissance era. Basic musical elements such as the division of meters and the relationship of subdivided beats require a mathematical understanding. Concepts in science such as humidity, fluid dynamics, and physics can be integrated with instrument knowledge such as woodwind care and sound wave properties.

Current Trends and Issues in Music Education

Role of Music Education in Cultural Diversity

As the United States becomes increasingly multicultural and diverse, the role of music education is adjusting its aim to encompass music and cultures from around the world. Music education in the United States has historically focused on the music of the Western world, such as Western classical music, American band music, and Western folk traditions. As more and more students in the American classroom come from diverse backgrounds, music educators should incorporate more **world music** within the curriculum. Elementary music teachers can use Latin, South African, Indian, Chinese, and Japanese music, among others, to illustrate basic arts standards such as singing in groups and learning musical elements. Band, choral, and orchestra directors should include non-Western musical repertoire in concerts, such as those of non-Western composers and arrangers. As the ethnic makeup of the student population diversifies, so too should music education diversify to reflect the multicultural aspect of modern society.

Non-Formal Teaching and Informal Learning

In contrast to a formal learning setting in which a music educator introduces educational content to a student, informal training refers to a student's **self-led** exploration of musical learning with or without an experienced mentor. Non-formal teaching and informal learning can constitute a valuable part of the student's growth as a musician. When students are in charge of their own musical development, they are able to choose the style and direction of their growth. This casual form of learning gives students more **autonomy** in their education, which encourages them to become more involved in their own learning. Many famous musicians were self-taught, and students can learn what works best for them as individuals, instead of a teacher-dictated method or form. However, educators should be careful about the potential **pitfalls** of disregarding formal education entirely for non-formal teaching. Since a student is entirely accountable for his or her own musical development, educational outcomes can be highly variable depending on the student. Also, students who learn informally tend to practice only those skills that are their strengths, while their weaker skills are neglected.

Using Adaptive Technology for Helping Students with Disabilities

The modern music classroom has paved the way for inclusive learning for students with disabilities. The use of **adaptive or assistive technology** allows students with disabilities or injuries the opportunity for music education and achievement. Many iPad applications act as a touch-sensitive synthesizer to convert movement to audio, allowing students with limited mobility or digits to create music. If a visually impaired student must move between instruments, the use of a simple string to guide the student can greatly widen the possibilities for performance. Also, sheet music can be enlarged for students with low vision, or even translated to Braille for students who are blind. For students who have trouble holding an instrument or reaching all the keys, music educators can use adaptive toggles, joysticks, clamps, and other tools to allow the student to be able to play. Students who are hard of hearing can use cochlear implants, hearing aids, or vibration-based technologies to play in an ensemble.

Utilitarian Approach to the Philosophy of Music Education

The utilitarian philosophy for the inclusion of music in general educational curriculum stems from the writings of Plato and Aristotle in ancient Greece. Good character, civic responsibility, cultural awareness, and a quality of nobility were only some of the noted non-musical benefits of music study. For music educators who embrace a **utilitarian philosophy** of music education, music is a tool to develop extra-musical benefits, whether in other intellectual fields, for the development of character, or for social entertainment. Arguments in favor of this utilitarian philosophy point to the persistence, control, and aural awareness students need in order to develop musical performance skills. Students develop fine motor skills when executing instrumental performance. Comprehension skills are reinforced when students master various levels of musical complexity. Singing helps students develop deep breathing and a strong diaphragm. For supporters of a utilitarian rationale, music is a key component of a **comprehensive education**.

Aesthetic Approach to the Philosophy of Music Education

The aesthetic philosophy for the inclusion of music in the general curriculum emerged during the national education reform of the 1950s. As schools sought to redefine general education in the US, music educators saw the need for a new philosophy of music education beyond what the utilitarian philosophy could provide. Influential theorists of **aesthetic arts education** include Bennett Reimer, Michael Mark, Elliot Eisner, Charles Leonhard, Robert House, and Maxine Greene. These scholars argued that music ought to be studied in and for itself; only through music and the arts can students develop the sensitivity, feeling, and symbolic communication represented by musical understanding. Any extra-musical benefits pale in comparison to the pure **enjoyment** and interaction of making music. To supporters of the aesthetic philosophy for the inclusion of music education, no other field of study can develop the musical perception, mental sensations, and appreciation for beautiful sound except music study itself.

Collaboration in Music Education

Collaborating with Colleagues

Music education cannot exist in isolation. A single instructor, though dedicated and focused in delivering a high-quality curriculum, cannot meet the educational demands of all the students alone. **Collaboration** is advantageous in music education for various reasons. When collaborating with veteran colleagues, a music teacher can learn valuable **educational strategies** that only come with long-term experience. Music selection, behavior management, and instructional assessment are all areas that a willing, humble, and open collaboration can enhance. Students will also benefit when music teachers collaborate with instructors from other school subjects, whether math, English, or history. When educational objectives are **reinforced** within another classroom, learning is heightened, and the students learn that no one subject exists in the world in isolation; everything is interconnected. A music educator can also collaborate with the school librarian in asking for current resources, and the librarian can better understand what materials are needed to best supply the music department. Every individual has a unique set of strengths and talents; by collaborating with colleagues, the music curriculum can become an inspired agent for student transformation.

Review Video: Collaborating with Other Professionals
Visit mometrix.com/academy and enter code: 100351

IEPs

According to the **Individuals with Disabilities Education Act**, schools must provide students who have learning disabilities with the same educational opportunities as their typically developing classmates. After the initial assessment, a unique educational program is developed for each student with special needs, called the **Individualized Education Program** (IEP). The IEP outlines educational goals and other services or strategies needed for the student to achieve those goals. As a music educator, involvement with support staff and faculty regarding a student's IEP greatly enhances the quality of music education a student with special needs receives. The more a music educator understands a student's learning disability and techniques to aid musical learning, the more the student can engage in musical development. The music educator can collaborate with music therapists, special education teachers, and school counselors to better design special educational programs and receive consultant, direct service, and in-service assistance.

Review Video: Medical Conditions in Education
Visit mometrix.com/academy and enter code: 531058

Review Video: History and Foundations of Special Education
Visit mometrix.com/academy and enter code: 100350

Parent-Teacher Conferences

Parental involvement is one of the most important factors in student success in school. When parents participate in their children's educational process, children learn from their most important support figures and gain encouragement, self-esteem, and a role model for a lifetime. One way music teachers can influence and nurture parental support in their students' education is through **parent-teacher conferences**. Many techniques for successful parent-teacher conferences can be used to open **two-way communication** in helping parents support their student's learning process. First, teachers must help parents be aware of conference dates and goals. Multiple announcements through various mediums and providing information in many different languages will help parents plan for conferences. Flexibility is key in planning sessions so that parents have the option of early morning, afternoon, or early evening times, as well as the option for extended sessions. Teachers can also coordinate free services through the PTA, such as transportation, childcare, and refreshments. Two-way communication can be achieved through providing opportunities for dialogue, flexibility, and an open and receptive attitude.

Student-Led Parent-Teacher Conferences

In recent years, there has been a trend toward student-led parent-teacher conferences. The rationale behind this method holds that when students step up as a catalyst for parent-teacher communication, students gain **accountability** for their educational development, awareness of the importance of open communication, and leadership skills, among other benefits. In the **student-led parent-teacher conference model**, teachers act as facilitators while students are responsible for answering any teacher or parent questions pertaining to academic achievement, student portfolios, educational development, and grades and assessment. Some teachers have students fill out **self-assessment surveys** before a conference to help students evaluate their learning, their strengths, weaknesses, skills, and habits, and their social interaction with classmates. This approach to parent-teacher conferences helps parents see their children taking initiative for their own educational process, and helps to transfer that open communication during conferences to the home environment.

Chapter Quiz

Ready to see how well you retained what you just read? Scan the QR code to go directly to the chapter quiz interface for this study guide. If you're using a computer, simply visit the online resources page at **mometrix.com/resources719/nesincmusic** and click the Chapter Quizzes link.

Preparing for Rehearsal and Performance

CONDUCTING

BASIC ELEMENTS OF CONDUCTING TECHNIQUE

As the leader of a group of musicians, the conductor plays an essential role in making music throughout performance or rehearsals. Several key elements of conducting technique play a vital role in coordinating various musical elements into one collective effort. At the most basic level, the conductor indicates the tempo and the meter; the conductor must have a clear beat pattern that indicates not only a steady tempo, but also the meter of the music. The conductor must also indicate **preparatory beats** for certain sectional or instrumental entrances as well as releases at the end of a section or phrase. Conductors also indicate **fermatas**, changes in tempo, and dynamics. The conductor must also actively listen to the balance between sections and present the right cues to maintain dynamics and the proper balance. Other essential elements of conducting technique include style-specific musical interpretation, the role of the free hand, and score study.

CONDUCTING PATTERNS

In a **2/4 pattern**, the hand moves downward on the first beat and upward on the second beat. In a **3/4 pattern**, the hand moves downward on the first beat, outward on the second beat, and upward on the third beat. In a **4/4 pattern**, the hand moves downward on the first beat, inward on the second beat, outward on the third beat, and upward on the fourth beat. In a **compound 6/8 pattern**, the hand moves downward on the first primary strong beat, bounces inward on the second and third beats, moves outward on the secondary strong fourth beat, bounces outward on the fifth beat, and upwards on the sixth beat. In a **compound 9/8 pattern**, the hand moves downward on the first primary strong beat, bounces inward on the second and third beats, moves outward on the secondary strong fourth beat, bounces outward on the fifth and sixth beats, then moves upward on the tertiary strong seventh beat, and bounces upward and inward on the weak eighth and ninth beats.

GENERAL PRINCIPLES FOR CONDUCTING BEAT PATTERNS

When conducting certain beat pattern, there are several principles to keep in mind. The **downbeat** of the pattern always indicates the strongest pulse of the pattern, and it is indicated by a downward stroke of the hand. Also, the last beat of the pattern is always the **weakest pulse** of the pattern and is thus indicated by an upward stroke of the hand. If in a compound meter there exists a secondary strong pulse, then the movement of the hand is almost just as strong of a downbeat as the primary strong downbeat. The movement of the hand in a three- or four-beat pattern moves so that collisions between the baton hand and the free hand are avoided. Conductors may choose to indicate **subdivided pulses** such as eight pulses in a slow 4/4 movement, or to indicate fewer pulses in a fast movement, such as conducting only the downbeats of a fast 3/4 waltz.

POSITION OF THE BATON AND THE VARIOUS ROLES OF THE FREE HAND

When conducting, the position of the baton should be a natural extension of the hand and arm. It should not be rigidly in line, but should serve as a musical tool of expression; in a gentle passage, the **baton** may be lightly held with only the first few fingers, but in an animated passage, the baton may be tightly grasped to evoke a feeling of passion and urgency. The elbow should be slightly raised away from the body so that the baton can be clearly seen from all angles. The **free hand** without the baton plays the role of musical reinforcement and can also help turn pages. As an independent stimulus, the free hand can reinforce dynamics such as crescendos and decrescendos, as well as aid in cueing parts. The free hand should also indicate releases, phrasing, musical style, and necessary modifications in the balance of the ensemble.

Posture While Conducting

When conducting an ensemble, careful attention should be made to bodily posture so that no slight imbalance or awkward position will detract from the clear musical cues from the conductor. The conductor's feet should be about shoulder width with one foot slightly more forward to maintain optimal balance. The knees should not bend, and equal weight should be given to each foot. The conductor's spine should be tall and erect. Just before beginning, the arms should be in an attention position using both the baton hand and the free hand held ready to indicate the preparatory beat. The arms should not be too close to the body and should be held up and out at a comfortable width. The elbows should be slightly forward ready to engage the ensemble. The wrists should be flexible and neither limp nor stiff.

Determining the Number of Beats to Conduct Based on Tempo

Though there are standard beat patterns in the art of conducting technique, the pattern that conductors choose to conduct should be determined by tempo, style, and meter. In a 2/4 meter, the conductor could indicate every beat; if the 2/4 meter is taken at vivace, however, it would be impractical to conduct every beat, and an indication of the downbeat would suffice. Excessive movements could convey heaviness, which could slow down the ensemble. If, however, the 2/4 meter is taken at adagio, the conductor could facilitate rhythmic fluidity and continuity by doubling the number of beats, indicating the quarter-note subdivision for a 4/4 beat pattern, so that forward movement is not lost. In general, the faster the tempo, the fewer number of beats the conductor should indicate; the slower the tempo, the higher number of beats the conductor should indicate.

Giving a Clear Attack

It is of utmost importance to provide a clear attack while conducting an ensemble. Without a precise indication of the ictus, the ensemble will not begin to play the music together and may continue to approximate the tempi and rhythms, resulting in a disorderly performance. To give a **clear attack** in conducting, the conductor must give a preparatory beat. During this imaginary preceding beat, the arm must move fluidly in exactly the same tempo as the intended beginning tempo; this way, the musician can easily judge the preparation movement and downbeat. The conductor should breathe in on the preparatory beat along with the ensemble and indicate the attack with equally suggestive bodily language such as direct eye contact and a head nod. The conductor must be careful to place gestural emphasis on the attack and only a slight movement on the preparatory beat.

Indicating a Fermata

When conducting a fermata, several considerations should be made: the tempo and presence or absence of a ritardando, the length of the fermata, the presence or absence of a rest after the fermata, and resuming tempo if the music continues. If the **fermata** is on the last note of the piece, the conductor should gesture in a circular motion downward as long as the fermata is to be held. If the music continues after a fermata without a break, the conductor should gesture slightly outward and upward to incorporate the preparation beat for the next note. If the music continues after a fermata with a rest, the conductor should indicate a cutoff and resume with the preparation beat in the intended tempo of the next section. Effort should be made to eliminate any awkward movements so that the musicians can comfortably play a fermata for the length indicated.

Creating a Clean Release

In conducting, the release of a note is as important as the initial attack; clear indication must be made on the conductor's part so that the musician does not have any doubt when to release a note. When indicating a **release**, the conductor should also use a preparatory beat to indicate the cutoff. A release usually comes after holding a long note; as such, the conductor's baton should indicate the final note to be played, then be held in position for as long as the note is to be held with a possible slight movement outwards. The preparatory beat to indicate the release should be a slight movement upwards so as not to detract from the musical expression of the final note. As the conductor's baton comes down or out from the preparatory beat, the stress of the cutoff marks the point of the release.

Preparatory, Active, and Passive Beats

In conducting, there are several types of gestural indications: preparatory beats, active beats, and passive beats. Conductors use **preparatory beats** to ready an ensemble before an attack and before a release to allow the ensemble to anticipate the cutoff of a held note. Preparatory beats should indicate the tempo, style, and expression of the music to be played. Conductors use **active beats** to signal an immediate change or action from the ensemble. Typical changes that may be indicated by an active beat include marcato, legato, staccato, and accents. **Passive beats** are beats that do not require an immediate change from the ensemble but help to indicate things like rests, offbeats, and other simple pulses. The conscientious conductor should use all three types of beats in variation to elicit musical changes such as sectional transitions, syncopations, hemiolas, and other important musical events.

Influence of the Conductor on an Ensemble

In addition to coordinating the rhythmic timing of players and other musical logistics, part of the conductor's role is to establish the emotional content and **musical expression** of the performance. A skilled conductor is able to extract the appropriate musical expression from the ensemble with the slightest of gestures. The conductor should utilize his or her entire body in conveying the musical expression of the piece. An energetic musical section might require the conductor to exaggerate movements in a quicker manner, with an animated expression on the face, to draw out a similar energetic mood from the players. Likewise, a somber musical section might require the conductor to conduct with heavier, slower movements, with a grave expression on the face, to draw out a similar dark and solemn sound from the players.

Techniques Conveying Dynamics and Expression

The conductor's role in directing an ensemble encompasses all musical interpretation, from tempo and balance to dynamics and expression. As such, a conductor's technique greatly influences an ensemble's performance of a musical piece. When indicating a forte or fortissimo, the conductor's gestures should be similarly bigger and "louder." The conductor can use the free hand to aid in ensemble response by signaling for more. When indicating a piano or pianissimo, the conductor's gestures should be similarly smaller and "softer." The conductor can use the free hand to aid in ensemble response by signaling for less. **Body language** plays an important part in eliciting dynamic and expressive contrast from the ensemble. A forte gesture can be made passionately sorrowful with heavy movements in the arms and a somber expression in the face; likewise, a forte can be made joyful and exuberant with light movements in the arms and lifted eyebrows in the face.

Studying a Score to Conduct

Studying Recordings

The use of other recordings as part of **score study** has certain advantages and disadvantages. An unfamiliar piece of music may be quickly understood through listening to an existing performance. If the conductor is developing his or her own interpretation of the music, this may be informative in terms of tempo and style; however, this may also contribute to a "parrot" interpretation where the conductor has not made his or her own in-depth interpretation. Also, this may lead to other imitated musical characteristics that may not be historically or stylistically accurate, as every performance is framed by the conductor's interpretation. Thus, using recordings in score study can be an informative source of past interpretations but should not become an exact template from which to copy.

When using recordings in score study, careful discretion must be made so that the conductor does not merely copy the interpretation of the recording. Several techniques can be applied when using recordings to prevent a "parrot" version of an existing performance. The conductor should listen to more than one interpretation of a piece to have a wide variety of interpretations. Also, the conductor should not practice conducting to the recording, as muscle memory can impede the personal development of the conductor's own interpretation. The conductor should not adhere only to famous recordings or famous conductors; effort should be made to listen to a variety of lesser-known recordings. Another helpful technique is to listen early in the score study and then stop once rehearsals have begun to be able to more fully develop one's own interpretation.

Learning Musical Aspects

As a conductor, one of the foremost responsibilities in leading an ensemble musically is having an in-depth understanding of the music. One of the musical aspects a conductor should know scrupulously is the **instrumentation** and **transpositions** of the scored instruments. Another important musical facet to know is the **form** of the work; knowing the form will generate a deeper understanding of the development of the theme. Special attention should be given to analyze the harmonic and melodic structure of the work. The conductor can then easily listen to the **balance** of the ensemble. The conductor should also know the dynamics of the score to be able to prepare the ensemble to execute changes in sound. Finally, the conductor must study the phrase structure and any other special instrument execution.

Techniques Used to Learn a Score

Through score study, the conductor must analyze, reanalyze, interpret, and learn every detail and nuance in the music. There are several techniques that can aid the conductor in score study. During the learning process, the conductor can play all the **vocal parts** together on the piano to be able to listen to voice leading and harmonic changes. The conductor can also play the **accompaniment part** separately on the piano so that special attention can be given to the accompaniment when the entire ensemble plays. If there is text, the conductor can read the text aloud, poetically, so as to examine the ideal **dramatic inflection** and stress of the line. The conductor should analyze the score structurally, harmonically, dynamically, and melodically to know the music thoroughly. The conductor can also mark the score extensively to help mentally note all aspects of the music.

Resources for Score Research

When studying the score, there are several useful resources the conductor can use. For a thorough understanding of the historical background and performance practices, conductors can refer to scholarly books, journals, and articles to research the background of the musical work. Many musical works also have ties to extra-musical art forms such as literature, dance, visual art, and theater. Researching these sources of musical inspiration will aid the conductor's interpretation and understanding of the score. The conductor can also use recordings of the musical work to research performance practices and stylistic differences of past performances. If the musical work was written by a living composer, the conductor may also interview the composer to delve deeper into a thorough understanding of the score. Also, consulting conducting texts can also provide relevant perspectives on the musical score.

Musical Elements Involved Musical Interpretation

The role of conductor as musical interpreter requires adept conducting technique and a solid conviction of his or her own understanding of the music. In forming an **interpretation** of the music, the conductor must consider the stylistic elements of the music. Note durations, stresses, tempo, articulation, phrasing, dynamics, and other nuances all make up the necessary musical elements for a conductor to direct an ensemble well. Additionally, the conductor's own **vision** of the musical work should be made clear through the ensemble's performance. The conductor's understanding of the progression of the music (its beginnings, climaxes, and endings) should inform the execution of all musical elements. The conductor should understand the historical background of the music as well as the essence of the music itself. Interpretation takes creativity, imagination, musical flexibility, and an intimate understanding of the emotions of the music.

Musical Elements Important in Score Marking

In preparation for rehearsing a musical work, the conductor should mark the score for his or her own benefit; this saves time as well as processing energy when in rehearsals. During score study, the conductor should **mark** any or all of the following elements to prepare for the rehearsal process: entrances of sections, entrances of melodies and important themes, tutti sections, dynamic changes, fermatas, repeats, cadenzas, meter changes, tempo changes, sectional changes, harmonic structure, melodic structure, rhythmic structure, form, textual emphases, instrumentation changes, key changes, balance changes, style indications, free-hand cues, fermatas, and special preparatory beats. It may not be necessary to mark every change in the music; however, the score should be marked to the needs of each conductor to ensure a thorough analysis of the musical score.

Using Ostinato in Accompaniment

An ostinato is defined as a short, repeating accompaniment pattern throughout a musical work that can consist of a simple rhythmic, melodic, or harmonic idea. Similar to a drone, the **ostinato** provides a stable foundation for the main melody line(s). In terms of improvisation, the ostinato is a practical tool for creating new ideas and melodies as the repeated figures stay constant, allowing the melody line to focus on a free delivery. When an ostinato is used in Baroque music, it is termed the **basso ostinato**, or ground bass, and can feature both harmonic and melodic properties. When an ostinato is used in jazz music, it is termed the **riff** or vamp, and helps to form the framework for a tune. Ostinatos are also found extensively in world music such as that of Africa and India.

Using Arpeggiation in Accompaniment

An arpeggio is defined as a chord that is played note by note, successively instead of simultaneously. Also termed a broken chord, the **arpeggio** can be played from the highest note to the lowest note, but is more commonly played from the lowest note to the highest note. When using arpeggiation in accompaniment, the musician plays individual chords as arpeggios. If accompanying a single instrument, arpeggiation can be a practical musical technique as the arpeggio fills out the texture of the sound and adds forward motion to the music, as the chords become single notes flowing through one another instead of a simple blocked chord that must be sustained. Arpeggios also tend to soften the delivery of the accompaniment, giving the music a sense of lightness such as that of arpeggiated harp music.

Using Blocked Chords in Accompaniment

Blocked chords are defined as pitches that are played simultaneously like a chord. When using blocked chords in accompaniment, the player can combine notes that are written separately into a **blocked chord**, or play blocked chords from a chord chart. If the player must sight-read music, blocking the chords can help to simplify the sight-reading process so that the player doesn't have to read every single note; a quick scan of the harmony is all that is required to play a blocked chord of that harmony. If the player is reading music with a chord chart, then blocking chords can also provide a quick and simple method of accompaniment. In this case, the player only needs to see the written harmony to play the blocked harmony without the intermediate processing stage of notation.

Publicizing Music Programs and Events

In a music program, there is usually a limited budget for yearly expenses; music educators can stretch the program budget by implementing cost-effective methods of publicizing music programs and events. One area in which the music educator can minimize cost is through **concert publications**. Instead of using costly printed posters, the music educator can take advantage of **social media**, publicizing upcoming events through the Internet instead of through paper. If the program still needs paper publications, the music educator can use smaller flyers that will cost less than larger posters. The music educator can also publicize music programs through the help of a **parent committee**; working as a team, supporters of the music program can publicize upcoming concerts and events through fundraising efforts while also spreading information about the program. The music educator may also eliminate the cost of program notes by having an announcer give brief introductory information between musical works.

Preparing Program Notes for a Performance Setting

Preparation for program notes involves extensive and thorough research on the musical work as well as its historical context and contextual background. When first starting to research, it is important to consult a variety of sources for the most accurate information. A good starting point for any music research is the *New Grove Dictionary of Music and Musicians*. As a standard, authoritative text, this source offers the most up-to-date and complete resource available. After consulting the *New Grove Dictionary*, it is useful to use composer biographies, orchestral music resources, CD liner notes, primary notes on the score, and other published collections of program notes. The writer should also check the text and translations for the most accurate rendering. Once researched, the **program notes** should be written, including historical, biographical, and contextual information as well as information about the work itself.

Essential Elements Included in Program Notes

Program notes should serve as a helpful guide for the audience while listening to a musical performance. It should provide **key elements** to understanding the work, such as contextual background, historical context, first performance, scoring, musical style, and possible details to listen for. The writer should avoid personal anecdotes, footnotes, irrelevant facts and details, musical examples or excerpts, exclusively technical terminology, or effusive emotional descriptions. Program notes should be insightful and engaging, and they should further the enjoyment of the listening audience. While all program notes should be thoroughly researched, they must be geared toward the level of understanding of the audience (whether for a young audience or for expert theorists). If possible, the writer should include unique and engaging facts such as the initial reception through a first review or the dedication of the work.

Role of the Music Educator

As a leader of a student's music education, the music educator should be an advocate of proper **concert etiquette**. Although there are many aspects of music for a student to learn, it is equally important for a student to understand the proper way to act both as a concert musician as well as an audience member. As such, concert etiquette should be an integral part of every rehearsal and lesson. The student can begin practicing such performance etiquette as proper sitting or standing posture, as well as appropriate eye contact. The student can also begin to practice such things as entrance etiquette and bowing after performance. The students in the classroom can practice **good audience technique** through peer performance, exhibiting polite listening manners, withholding clapping between movements, and applause after a performance. The music educator can also take the opportunity during parent conferences or before a concert to address members of the audience regarding proper concert etiquette.

Appropriate Etiquette

Any audience member should be aware of the performance venue for a concert, as there are different etiquettes for different performance venues. In a classical concert, the audience usually does not talk during a performance, as it is considered disruptive, and applause is only polite at the end of a musical work. In contrast, jazz audiences can often clap or give sound approval at any point of the performance to exhibit admiration for an improvised section or solo. At a rock concert, not only can the audience clap or give sound approval at any time, audience members can freely talk throughout the concert. Although the appropriate sound levels of the various audiences differ, some things remain constant at any venue. Audiences should arrive early to settle into the venue and feel comfortable. Audience members should always be aware of photography and videography regulations. Also, audiences are always responsible for their children at a concert.

Warm-Up and Performance Techniques

Breathing Warm-Up

Before beginning any choral rehearsal, it is essential for the director to prepare the singers both physically and mentally. One important aspect of warming up a choral ensemble is the breathing warm-up. **Breathing warm-ups** engage the diaphragm for supported singing and help to warm the vocal cords for singing. Not only will the breathing exercises physically prepare the lungs and vocal mechanisms for singing, they will also mentally center the singer to be mindful of breath during the rehearsal. One choral breathing warm-up consists of taking in a deep breath over as many counts as possible, holding the breath, and then slowly letting out the air on an "s" sound, over as many counts as possible. Another choral warm-up consists of having the singers exhale on a pulse with an open mouth "ha."

Instrumental and Choral Warm Up

Warming up serves several important physical and mental functions for the group ensemble. Mentally, it has the effect of centering and adjusting the ensemble to an appropriate mental state for performance and establishing proper physiological cues for posture, breathing, etc. **Warm-ups** serve as a unifying tool for all members of the ensemble to begin listening to each other as a musical entity and adjusting sound according to the group. Physically, the warm-up promotes blood flow to the entire body, making every member ready to respond to the physical demands of making music. Though easy to overlook, the warm-up serves an important function for the instrument as well as the body. Whether a brass, woodwind, string, percussion, or vocal instrument, every instrument should be properly warmed and its mechanisms stretched and lubricated. Without a proper warm-up, singers could damage their vocal mechanisms, and the tonal quality of instruments could suffer.

Correct Use of Breath in Singing

For any singer, the breath plays an essential role in producing a controlled, robust tone while keeping the vocal cords in good health. To begin any breath, the singer must inhale; the inhalation should be deep and initiated by the contraction of the **diaphragm**, the muscle and tendon that runs along the bottom of the ribcage. As the diaphragm contracts and is actively engaged, it creates a vacuum in the lungs, which begins the intake of oxygen. After the intentional inhalation, the singer must control the rate of exhalation, as the flow of air through the vocal cords results in sound. The singer must use great care not to allow the chest to collapse while managing the rate of airflow by engaging the abdominal muscles to achieve a steady stream of air through the trachea and larynx.

Long Tones for Brass Players

Long tones are a critical practice for brass and woodwind players. The benefit of the exercise lies in removing other aspects of performance such as reading, fingering, and so on. This allows the player to singly direct his or her focus toward the production of those aspects that create a pleasing tone. The definition of "pleasing tone" may vary according to the personal preference and the idiom of performance; however, **long tones** allow the performer to scrutinize and adjust pitch, timbre, vibrato, etc. Although the exercise has the additional benefit of increasing stamina and strength of the muscles involved, maximum duration of the held note should not be the sole or primary focus of long-note practice. Instead, the performer's attention should focus on the quality of the note through the coordination of the entire system that produces the note: diaphragm, throat, oral and sinus cavities, embouchure, and the instrument.

Physical Warm-Ups to Prepare the Chorus for Singing

Before beginning any choral rehearsal, it is essential for the director to prepare the singers both physically and mentally. The use of **physical warm-ups** helps the body to release any tension that may hinder the vocal delivery while also increasing blood flow to the vocal mechanisms. A useful physical warm-up to prepare the lips for singing consists of taking in a deep breath and releasing it through slack lips, as in a lip trill. Another helpful warm-up to prepare the mouth for singing consists of stretching the mouth wide open while imitating the chewing motion. Singers must also stretch appropriately before singing to help loosen the neck and shoulder muscles through shoulder rolls, neck rolls, side bends, and arm extensions. Singers can also take in deep breaths, and release them as heavy sighs while dropping the shoulders to help loosen the body.

Ideal Posture for Singing

The ideal posture for singing should engage the entire body while avoiding any tension or restrictions on the vocal mechanisms. The feet should be shoulder-width apart, with one foot slightly in front of the other for optimal balance. The weight of the body should lean slightly forward instead of backwards on the heels. The knees should be loose and never locked. The hands should be relaxed and kept by the side of the body or engaged in expressing a vocal line. The abdomen should be active and involved in supporting the breath. The arms and shoulders should be relaxed and allowed to hang freely. The chest should not be collapsed, but should be held high to support the breath. The singer's chin should be held level to the floor so as not to obstruct the flow of air through the trachea.

Vocalization Warm-Ups for Choirs

Before beginning any choral rehearsal, it is essential for the director to prepare the singers both physically and mentally through vocalization warm-ups. One such warm-up is the **siren**, in which all the singers sing to the upper reaches of their vocal range and slide back down to their lower reaches. Another warm-up consists of singing **pentatonic scales** upwards and downwards using consonant- and vowel-heavy sentences such as "Mommy Made Me Mash My M&Ms." Choruses can also warm up by sliding their voices from a Do to a Sol and back down. Yet another warm-up consists of singing Do to the next Do an octave up, back down to Sol-Mi-Do. A warm-up useful for vowels consists of singing a single pitch through the five vowels from open to close, or vice versa: "ee," "eh," "ah," "oh," and "oo."

Warming Up on Wind Instruments

Warming up serves several important physical and mental functions for the wind instrumentalist. Mentally, it has the effect of **centering** and adjusting the player to an appropriate mental state for performance and establishing proper physiological cues for posture, breathing, and more before the performance itself. In addition to establishing the mindset for performance, the warm-up provides necessary functions at a physical level. The warm-up promotes blood flow to the fingers and the structures associated with **embouchure**, making them feel "loose" and ready to respond to the demands of playing. Though easy to overlook, the warm-up serves an important function for the instrument as well as the body. An instrument that has been sitting in an air-conditioned room is significantly colder than it will be during a performance. The warm air of the player's breath passing through the instrument will create warmth and thus expansion. An instrument should either be warm before tuning or re-tuned after a thorough warm-up.

Using Solfège in Kinesthetic Pitch Learning

Solfège, also known as solfeggio in Italian, originated in the 17th century as a vocal exercise using solmization syllables for singing the pitches of a scale. **Solmization systems** were found all around the world, but the most commonly used one in Western culture stems from the Guidonian system of the 11th century. In teaching pitch names and associations, the use of solfège can greatly aid the student's understanding of high and low pitch. Educators such as John Curwen and Zoltán Kodály have integrated a kinesthetic system using both hand signs and spatial reasoning. The solmization for the diatonic scale, from tonic to tonic, is as follows: do, re, mi, fa, sol, la, si (ti), do. As each pitch rises, the corresponding hand sign also rises from the low on the body to high above the head. The spatial, kinesthetic association allows the learner to relate the rising pitch to rising motion.

Instrumental Rehearsal

Advantages and Disadvantages for Tuning Each Instrument

For conductors rehearsing a beginning ensemble, helping to tune the students' instruments can save time and confusion for the students. Especially with beginner students who are still familiarizing themselves with an instrument, having help with tuning will not only save time, but also offer an opportunity to teach the student how to tune. Although tuning each student's instrument has many advantages, there are also certain disadvantages to be aware of. If possible, the conductor should tune each student's instrument before the beginning of the rehearsal; otherwise, the time taken may be inefficient and detract from the limited rehearsal time. Also, if tuning instruments for middle school or high school students, care must be taken to encourage every student's own ability to tune; otherwise, tuning students' instruments for the sake of time may become a hindrance in the student's comprehensive music education.

Using Intonation Spot Checks of Different Sections During a Rehearsal

During a rehearsal, the director should use various techniques to ensure the accurate intonation of the ensemble. Aside from beginning each rehearsal with accurate tuning, the director can use spot checks of each different section as teaching moments as well. Isolating the instrument or vocal groups for intonation spot checks teaches the students to listen attentively to themselves and also to the surrounding students. Students will have opportunities to practice the appropriate procedures of adjusting pitch on their respective instruments. Brass instruments with slides can adjust their pitches through their slides; woodwinds can adjust their pitches through adjustments of the mouthpieces; string instruments can adjust their pitches through tuning pegs; vocalists can adjust their pitches through minor adjustments of their vocal mechanisms. When participating in intonation spot checks, students will learn to produce a consistent pitch with their breath or their open strings.

Proper Brass Embouchure for Good Tone Quality

For brass instruments, proper brass embouchure and good air support directly affect tone quality. The player must provide consistent breath support through deep inhalations, controlled exhalations, and a relaxed body. Once the player has a good breath foundation, proper **embouchure** must also be practiced for tone quality, intonation, endurance, range, and articulation. For the brass player, the lips are the source of a sound wave's motion and energy; the mouth cavity should be wide and open while the lips touch together as if saying "M." When the player **buzzes**, the lips should stay relaxed while the corners of the lips should stay firm, not too tight or too loose. The player should keep the chin even and pointed. As a general guideline, the player should keep the mouthpiece equally held between the two lips.

Tuning Strategies in an Instrumental Rehearsal

There are a variety of tuning strategies for tuning an instrumental ensemble for rehearsal. For a beginning ensemble, the conductor may tune each student's instrument, preferably before the rehearsal starts, or quickly and efficiently at the beginning of the rehearsal. If the ensemble is at a level of playing that requires proper tuning abilities, the ensemble may tune based on the pitch of the lead oboe or lead clarinet playing the concert pitch. The conductor can also choose to have each section tune as a group at the beginning of rehearsal, so that musicians can match the pitch and timbre of the instrumental section. Also, musicians can tune based on a tuning machine that plays a pure tone concert pitch where the musicians must listen carefully to adjust their instruments to the proper pitch.

Tuning an Ensemble Upwards from the Bass

One method of tuning an ensemble starts with careful tuning upwards from the bass. In a choir, this would be the lowest bass voices; in an orchestra, this would be the basses, cellos, bass clarinets, bassoons, trombones, and tubas. In a concert band or wind ensemble, this would be the bassoons, bass clarinets, trombones, tubas, bass saxophones, and euphoniums. Once the bass instruments have been carefully and precisely tuned, the next instruments higher in range would be tuned, and so on and so forth, until the entire ensemble has been tuned through the bass, middle, and soprano ranges. The theory behind this tuning method holds that with precise tuning, the other instruments can more easily hear their tuning pitches because of the overtones and harmonics from the bass sounds. Also, the other instruments can more easily place their pitches within the context of a chord structure, as the bass becomes the foundational pitch of the ensemble.

Lifting the Palate in Vocal Technique

The **soft palate**, also called the velum, is the soft tissue at the top of the mouth cavity that rises and lowers as the mouth swallows and in speech. The soft palate is responsible for closing off the nasal cavity while the mouth swallows so that any material in the oral cavity proceeds to the esophagus. In vocal technique, singers practice singing with an open throat where the velum is raised and the larynx is lowered. This allows the sound quality to be more relaxed and free while also easing register transitions and maintaining the health of the vocal mechanisms. When singers lift the soft palate, the resulting space within the oral cavity enlarges, helping to achieve a more resonant, warm tone without restrictions. Since this action also relaxes the surrounding vocal muscles, the singer can transition between registers more easily, resulting in a consistently smooth tone.

Vocal Techniques to Achieve Vowel Uniformity

Vowel uniformity is an important aspect of singing, but it becomes all the more important within a chorus setting, as there are a multitude of various timbres, ranges, and singers contributing to a unified, homogenous sound. Each singer should practice certain vocal techniques to assist in keeping each vowel sound as uniform as possible. The mouth should be **open long** instead of wide, with the jaw falling low to open the oral cavity. The resulting vowels will be more open and resonant for better choral blend. The singers should also sing with an open throat while lifting the soft palate for a more relaxed and smoother sound. Also, the singer should not "swallow" his or her sound, but should direct the sound forward in the head so that the chorus can achieve a uniform, vibrant sound.

Techniques to Improve Poor Singing Posture

When singing, it is imperative to execute a healthy, proper singing posture not only for better ease in creating resonant sounds, but also for the health of the body. When the singer is standing, the weight of the body should be distributed evenly to all sides of the feet: front, back, side, and middle. The spine should be erect with the shoulders back and the neck held high. The head should not angle forward or backward, but should be kept in a neutral position so that airflow through the body has no restrictions, and so the singer's body does not sustain unnecessary fatigue. When the singer is sitting, the feet should be flat on the ground with the spine erect and aligned with the neck, shoulders, head, and ears. The body should be balanced and relaxed through the entire vocal session.

Instructional Strategies for Different Class Settings

Comprehensive Outline of a Regular Full Ensemble Rehearsal

In a regular full ensemble rehearsal, the conductor or director should prepare a **comprehensive plan** for the time with the ensemble. Since rehearsal time is usually limited, the conductor should prioritize the musical goals for the session beforehand. The sequencing of the rehearsal goals is up to the conductor, based on the musical works and ensemble, but every rehearsal should have the same general components. In the beginning, the ensemble should spend adequate time warming up their instruments and bodies as well as tuning their instruments. This practice helps to develop both the musician's habits as well as listening with awareness. The ensemble should have time with the conducting and playing of various musical works. The ensemble should also spend time refining technically and musically challenging sections. There should also be time for the musicians to develop musicality and sight-reading during the rehearsal.

Sectional Rehearsals and Full Ensemble Rehearsals

Sectional rehearsals are an important tool for the rehearsing ensemble. When too much time is spent on an individual section or part during the full ensemble rehearsal, time is wasted and musicians can become unengaged. **Sectional rehearsals** allow players to fine-tune their parts together and to fix any technical or musical problems apart from the full ensemble. Sometimes the conductor may not be aware of other hidden problems except through listening to sectional rehearsals. However, certain precautions should be taken to ensure the highest efficiency of a sectional rehearsal. Sectionals should be scheduled either immediately before or after a full ensemble rehearsal; that way, the progress made through a sectional can be immediately integrated within the full ensemble for the most improvement. Players should also be aware of clear objectives before beginning any sectional to avoid wasting time.

Role of the Section Leader

As a section leader in a larger ensemble, there are several responsibilities that must be met to strengthen the musical excellence and unity of the performing group. The **section leader**, or principal of a section, should be thoroughly prepared with his or her own musical part, since this will be the framework for the rest of the section. The section leader should also be ready to give advice in terms of style, articulation, phrasing, bowing, fingering, and other musical details. The section leader should also be proficient at keeping accurate tuning and should help to ensure the proper intonation of the entire section. The section leader is also responsible for interpreting any directives the conductor may give concerning musical interpretation such as dynamics, phrasing, articulation, and character.

Individual Student Lessons

For any student in a large group ensemble, there can be many benefits for the student in taking additional individual lessons with a **private teacher**. Although a student can learn the basics solely through ensemble rehearsals, it is preferable for students to learn the basics with the help of a private teacher. In an ensemble rehearsal, the conductor can only give so much attention to an individual student, as there are many other students who may need help as well. With a private teacher, the student can have undivided help from a focused professional to guide the student's musical education, ensuring that proper technique and musicality are reinforced from the beginning. As the student progresses to a more advanced level, having a private teacher will better assist in technical challenges and fingering issues that cannot be addressed as easily in a large group ensemble. With a private teacher, a student can advance more quickly to a higher level of playing.

Selecting Music for an Ensemble

Each conductor has the final responsibility to select appropriate music for an ensemble. The conductor should consider the ability level of the ensemble; music should not be impossibly hard or too easy, but just challenging enough for the ensemble to be able to play the music while progressing both musically and technically. The conductor should also consider the strengths and weaknesses of the ensemble. The music should not always cater to an ensemble's strengths, but should also help to improve any weaknesses an ensemble may have. The conductor should also consider the number of players and instruments in the ensemble; minor changes can be made, but it is difficult to rearrange a full instrumentation to a few instruments. When selecting music, the conductor should also take into account the number of rehearsals before the given performance; there should be adequate time to rehearse any given piece. The conductor should also select a variety of music appropriate for the audience and occasion of the performance.

Teaching Rhythm to an Elementary Class

In a full elementary class, there are many important instructional strategies to effectively teach rhythm to young students. The students must first experience rhythm; this can be achieved through **kinesthetic movement**, whether by clapping, swaying the body, or dancing. The music educator can have students mimic certain clapping or dancing patterns so that the students experience the rhythms before labeling the rhythms. Students can also experience rhythms by keeping a beat to music, to help develop a feel for a steady beat. The music educator can refer to a steady beat as a heartbeat, relating it to a familiar internal process. Once students have experienced certain rhythms, the music educator can begin to assign visual and verbal labels to those rhythms. The association between label and rhythms can thus be strengthened, as the students already know the rhythms through experience.

Preventing Student Behavior Issues

When teaching a group of more than 15 students, certain strategies will benefit the educational environment. If there are instructions, they should clear and concise. When students understand instructions for a task, they are more likely to stay focused and on task. Follow the instructions with **reinforcement** by modeling the activity, asking the students to repeat the instructions back, or having the students do an example of the activity together, ensuring that students understand and can proceed with the activity. If instructions are not made clear, problems such as student frustration or loss of group control could occur. In addition, always establish rules, awards, and consequences for the classroom. It is essential that students have guidelines to operate within, so that when behavior issues do arise, the educator can act simply and according to guidelines rather than out of emotion.

Student Exhibiting Behavior Problems

When a student misbehaves in a classroom setting, it is always important for the music educator to reflect on the misbehavior. If an adjustment in teaching style or lesson sequencing will **redirect** the misbehavior, then the educator should start there. The teacher should also observe for any learning impairments that may trigger behavior problems. Also, the educator should make sure to set clear limits and boundaries of behavior. If the student is misbehaving regardless of various strategies of engaging teaching techniques and sequencing, then the educator should **address** the misbehavior, taking care not to condemn the student but rather the behavior. The music educator should make sure not to interrupt the flow of the lesson but to address the misbehaving student with as little verbal response as possible; the teacher can use silence, physical cues, close proximity, and quickly stating the student's name as reminders to focus. If these techniques are not effective, then the teacher should thoroughly address the misbehavior after class.

Keeping Students Focused and on Task

Keeping students focused and on task is one way to prevent behavior issues. There are many instructional strategies to refocus a misbehaving student. If students are distracted, wait until they are paying attention to continue the lesson. **Silence** will draw attention to the misbehaving students. If students are distracted, educators can **redirect** their attention by giving a direction such as "If you hear my voice, clap once." (Teachers may need to continue with clap twice, three times, etc.) Misbehaving students will redirect their attention and try not to be left out. Teachers can also **reward** good behavior through positive reinforcement. If needed, students should be separated. Establish a quieting signal such as raising a hand or two fingers. Teachers can also place a misbehaving student closer to themselves so that the student becomes conscious of his or her behavior among his classmates. Another technique is to give the misbehaving student a special task; oftentimes, a distracted student is one who is not challenged by the current lesson. Finally, if students continue misbehaving, the teacher may be talking too much, so adjustments may be needed to keep the students actively focused and involved.

Appropriate Classroom Objectives for Grades 5–8

Students in grades 5–8 should be reinforcing skills acquired in grades K-4, while preparing to achieve the standards set by the **National Achievement Standards** by grade 8. Students should be able to sing with expression from a variety of styles and genres by memory, on pitch, alone and in groups. Students should be able to perform on at least one instrument (alone as well as in groups) with good technique, posture, bowing or breath, and with good fingering. Students should be able to play simple tunes by ear. Students should also be able to improvise short melodies and simple accompaniment patterns. Students should be able to compose simple compositions in a variety of styles. Students should competently read treble and bass clefs, and whole, half, quarter, eighth, and sixteenth notes and rests in a variety of meters. Students should be able to analyze basic meter, rhythm, intervals, chords, and tonality. Students should also be able to relate music to history, other arts, and disciplines outside of music.

Sample Six-Week Curriculum and Objectives for Grades 1–2

In grades 1–2, students experience a wider range of musical characteristics, learning more about music by doing. Students should follow a balanced curriculum that includes **experiential learning** such as playing, singing, and moving to music. In a sample six-week curriculum that focuses on introducing rhythm to students, the first week might include games and songs that introduce the concept of a steady beat to students. In the second week, the concept of a steady beat should be reinforced while associating certain beats with certain counts (i.e., quarter note = 1 count, half note = 2 counts). In the third week, steady beat and notes should be reinforced through movement and songs. In the fourth week, the students should compose rhythms of quarter and half notes to music. In the fifth and sixth weeks, students should continue to reinforce these concepts as well as improvise on the learned rhythms through games, dance, and songs.

Establishing Classroom Rules

When teaching music in a group setting, it is always important to establish classroom rules and consequences in the beginning. The music educator should thoroughly explain **expectations** for the classrooms, detailing examples of good behavior and class participation. During this discussion, the music educator should also explain the **consequences** of inappropriate behavior or negative responses to rules so that the students know the system of classroom rules from the first day. Although **positive reinforcement** should be emphasized in classroom management, the educator may need to use **negative reinforcement** in certain situations. If a student responds negatively to classroom rules, the educator may try positive reinforcement first. If this is not effective, the teacher may have to remind the entire class of the rules and consequences. If this is not effective, then the teacher may have to talk individually to the student, reinforcing the rules and taking action on the consequences of not following the rules.

Every Pupil Responds Instructional Technique

Educators use the Every Pupil Responds instructional technique as a way to ensure student inclusion during a lesson. The technique requires students to simultaneously respond to the teacher's question by demonstrating or displaying the appropriate response. This allows the educator to quickly and efficiently check for understanding. The **Every Pupil Responds** technique can be adapted to fit a variety of situations and keeps students actively involved. Teachers can hand out cards with the answers "yes" or "no," different musical notational signs, or a blank board with which students can write their own responses to hold up. Additionally, teachers can instruct students to point to the correct object or placement on an instrument. If students are seated in pairs, teachers can instruct students to whisper the answer to their neighbor, and then have the entire classroom say the answer out loud.

Classroom Routines

Classroom procedures and routines are important for structure and organization within a student's day. Daily routines and procedures can also prevent many of the misbehaviors that result from an unorganized schedule and distractions. The lessons will have less interruption from distracted students and will flow much more easily. The music teacher should make sure to establish **clear procedures and routines** from the first day, taking care to go over each procedure in detail while modeling the procedures to ensure full understanding from the students. The first few weeks may require more time spent establishing procedures and routines, to help the rest of the school year flow more easily. Example classroom routines that are useful in providing structure and organization include how to enter the classroom, beginning work, roll call, announcements, "tardies," absences, teacher's attention signal, leaving one's seat, assignments, supplies, group work, and independent work.

Intrinsic Motivation in the Classroom

Intrinsic motivation is defined in behavioral psychology as motivation that exists for an individual in the activity itself, as opposed to extrinsic motivation in which motivation for an activity exists apart from the activity such as an outside pressure or reward. When students are **intrinsically motivated**, there will be satisfaction in the activity or task at hand, partly from a natural curiosity and partly from gratification in doing the task. Music educators can facilitate or encourage intrinsic motivation in the classroom; however, this type of motivation is only effective for those students who already have a natural tendency toward the task at hand. For other students who find no internal satisfaction or curiosity for the task at hand, intrinsic motivation may be useless. Intrinsic motivation, when effective, can foster a high quality of learning and creativity in students.

Extrinsic Motivation in the Classroom

Extrinsic motivation is defined in behavioral psychology as motivation that exists for an individual apart from the activity or task such as an outside pressure or reward, as opposed to intrinsic motivation in which motivation exists in the activity itself. When students are **extrinsically motivated**, satisfaction lies in an external reward, pressure, or some external prompt. Music educators can facilitate or encourage extrinsic motivation in the classroom, especially when there is a lack of intrinsic motivation. Oftentimes, the classroom structure is based on extrinsic motivation, through rewards such as grades, privileges, and peer esteem. Extrinsic motivation can also exist through a student's sense of future well-being and goals. If the music educator focuses on extrinsic motivators such as tangible rewards or a student's ego, the motivation will disappear when the motivators disappear. Thus, educators should encourage extrinsic motivators such as the student's acknowledgement of the tasks' importance toward a future goal.

Motivating Students in the Music Classroom

As a music educator, it is important to provide motivation for students in the music classroom, since motivated students result in higher engagement and better learning. One effective strategy for motivating students is to become a **role model** for the students; when the students see the excitement and passion for the lesson material, that energy will be transferred to the students. Another strategy is to get to know the students well; once the students know that the teacher is involved and invested in their education, they will be motivated to do well. Also, the teacher should use positive reinforcement and constructive criticism. These nonjudgmental remarks should motivate students with ways to improve. The music educator should also use frequent activities where the students have the opportunity to demonstrate their achievements, encouraging them to progress to the next level in cooperation. The teacher should also set **realistic performance goals**, ones that are appropriately challenging but still attainable.

National Core Arts Standards for Music

The National Core Arts Standards were developed to provide milestones to attain to on a grade-by-grade level in various forms of art, including dance, media arts, music, theatre, and visual arts. Usually, arts standards are dictated on the state and local level, but the national standards may be helpful in informing curriculum and instruction for a specific grade and art-subject. The **National Core Arts Standards** can be classified into these categories of artistic thought: creating, performing/presenting/producing, responding, and connecting. These categories of artistic thought are further subdivided into anchor standards, which inform the grade-level standards. The 11 anchor standards are as listed below:

Creating

- Generate and conceptualize artistic ideas and work.
- Organize and develop artistic ideas and work.
- Refine and complete artistic work.

Performing, Presenting, and Producing

- Select, analyze, and interpret artistic work for presentation.
- Develop and refine artistic techniques and work for presentation.
- Convey meaning through the presentation of artistic work.

Responding

- Perceive and analyze artistic work.
- Interpret intent and meaning in artistic work.
- Apply criteria to evaluate artistic work.

Connecting

- Synthesize and relate knowledge and personal experiences to make art.
- Relate artistic ideas and works with societal, cultural, and historical context to deepen understanding.

Care of Instruments

Care and Maintenance of Woodwind Instruments

Woodwind instrument should be handled with care, taking precaution to avoid damage by jewelry, buttons, or zippers. Instruments should be kept dry while in storage. After each playing session the instrument should be **wiped clean**, making sure to use an appropriately sized swab; this is especially important for the small-bored piccolo and oboe. On a monthly basis, **apply key oil** to key pivot points. Similarly, apply a small amount of **cork grease** to tenons and neck corks, taking care to remove any excess grease. Wipe down the finish of the instrument to remove fingerprints and oils from fingers, moisture, and other debris. Never use alcohol on any plastic parts, and never use excessive force when constructing the instrument. Thoroughly clean out the mouth between eating and playing; **clean mouthpieces** weekly. For reed instruments, **discard reeds** that are chipped or cracked; do not leave reeds on the mouthpiece, and check metal ligatures for signs of damage, as an out-of-round ligature can damage a mouthpiece. The instrument should be kept out of direct light and excessively warm, cold, or humid environments.

Care and Maintenance of Stringed Instruments

Stringed instruments require care and maintenance on several fronts. The instrument should be handled with care, and players should avoid directly handling the fragile **varnish**, which can be damaged by oils on the hands. When playing, care should be taken to avoid damage by jewelry, buttons, or zippers. Immediately after each use, remove oil, rosin dust, and other debris with a **soft cloth**. Special treated cloths can be used, but must not be used on strings or the hair of the bow. String instruments should, whenever possible, be kept in a well-regulated environment away from excessive exposure to direct light, too hot or too cold temperatures, and too dry or too humid environments. Failure to observe these precautions can result in bending, cracking, glue joint separations, arching distortion, and many other problems.

Care and Maintenance of Brass Instruments

Brass instruments require care and maintenance both inside and outside. Instruments should always be handled with care. Avoid handling the finish and wipe away any oil, dirt, or other debris with a soft cloth after handling. Be careful to avoid any damage from jewelry, buttons, or zippers. Before storage, use a **swab** to remove as much moisture as possible from the inside of the instrument, and remove the mouthpiece before storage. For valved instruments, apply a small amount of **valve oil** before each playing session. Clean and lubricate all slides, removing old lubricant before applying a new layer, and use only a small amount, removing any excess with a soft cloth. Whenever possible, keep the instrument in a cool environment that is neither too dry nor too humid. Perform a regular inspection of all moving parts and the mouthpiece.

Care and Maintenance of Percussion Instruments

Percussion instruments require regular maintenance and inspection depending on the specific percussion instrument involved. **Timpani** should be regularly inspected for an even and smooth head with a balanced action. On some timpani drums, the rim should be greased annually with lubricant such as cork grease, but others (like those that use Teflon tape) should never be lubricated; consult the manufacturer about specific care instructions regarding lubrication. Make sure to keep the timpani covered when not in use. **Metal mallet** instruments should be wiped regularly with a glass cleaner while **wooden bar** instruments should be wiped regularly with only a dampened cotton cloth or rag. Frequent inspections should be made to ensure that there are no splintered or cracked bars that need to be replaced. **Drums** should be maintained regularly through the cleaning and lubricating of the hardware. Periodically inspect the rim, counterhoop, and head for any serious issues that would warrant repair or replacement.

Involving Students in Caring for and Maintaining Orff Instruments

Regular care and maintenance of Orff instruments helps to prolong the life of the instruments. Music educators can involve students in the care and maintenance of the instruments for a learned sense of responsibility as well as an efficient method of cleaning the instruments. One example would be for the music educator to provide an end-of-the-year event that includes the cleaning of all **Orff instruments**. Students should remove the instrument bars and start with the vacuuming of all dust from the instrument. Next, the students should take a damp rag with an oil soap to wash and clean the boxes and wooden bars. After the instrument has been cleaned, the students can then take an oil polish (such as common furniture polish) to keep the instrument in proper, working condition. Music teachers can also have the students place a sticky note on any broken pins for the teacher to replace.

Professional Ethics and Legal Issues

Fair Use Provision in the 1976 Copyright Act

In the "fair use" provisions as set by the 1976 Copyright Act, educators are exempt from certain copyright laws, given the appropriate use and distribution of the copyrighted materials. When reproducing materials for use within the classroom, teachers are allowed to make **copies** of up to 10 percent of the entire work for each student, but cannot reproduce an entire copyrighted work for the classroom. When **recording** copyrighted materials, educators are exempt from the compulsory license only if the educator makes a single recording. If the educator wants to make more than one copy but fewer than 500, the educator should contact the publisher. To make more than 500 copies of the recording, the educator must obtain a license from an organization such as the **Harry Fox Agency**. The educator is allowed to rearrange a musical work in a reasonable way for educational purposes. The educator is allowed to **perform** a copyrighted song only if for demonstration in the classroom; all other performances require a license.

Licensing Resources

NMPA stands for the National Music Publishers' Association, which represents many of the music publishers in the United States and helps with copyright holder identification. The **MPA**, the Music Publishers' Association of the United States, similarly represents many print music publishers in the nation and also assists in copyright ownership issues. **ASCAP** (American Society of Composers, Authors, and Publishers), **BMI** (Broadcast Music, Inc.), and **SESAC** (Society of European Stage Authors and Composers) all function to exercise appropriate performance licensing and distribution to their publishers and members. The **HFA,** the Harry Fox Agency, primarily serves as a recording license resource for many of the US music publishers. The **US Copyright Office** is a part of the Library of Congress and provides general information on copyright laws and issues in the United States.

Maintaining Student Confidentiality and Appropriate Professional Conduct

Music educators are entrusted to oversee the growth, development, and well-being of the students. As such, they have certain moral and ethical obligations. The music educator should act in the highest professional manner with a commitment to the music education profession, to the students, to the community, and to family. Since music educators can be seen as **role models** to developing a student's musical growth, all **boundaries** between student and teacher should be honored so that both parties can be held above reproach. The music educator should act in a way that ensures an emotionally and physically safe and healthy environment for the students. When travelling to field trips and concerts, the students must ride in a district-approved vehicle and never in a personal vehicle. When greeting students, the teacher should exercise minimal physical contact, again, to be above reproach.

Music educators should obey all local, state, and federal **laws**, and should never put students in physical or emotional harm. When the music educator is in a non-school setting, he or she should continue to act with the highest level of judgment, since personal misconduct can lead to public disapproval and thus an interruption in the student's musical development and trust. Also, the music educator should never disclose a student's personal information to any person other than school personnel, or risk a confidentiality breach. The music educator should always maintain appropriate communication with the family, never for personal gain or advantage.

Professional Organizations and Resources

Professional Organizations for Music Educators

The **American String Teachers Association** is the largest professional organization for string teachers and offers journals, books, posters, and conferences, providing ongoing training for string teachers and promoting orchestra programs in schools and communities. The **Association of Teaching Artists** is a professional organization for "teaching artists" in all arts disciplines—music, dance, theater, visual arts, poetry, etc.—that provides a network and place for collaboration among all its members. The **Jazz Education Network** is a relatively new professional organization for jazz teachers, with conferences and festivals throughout the nation. The **Music Teachers National Association** is a professional organization supporting music teachers across the United States, providing conferences, festivals, and programs. The **National Association for Music Education** has 50 state affiliates and supports music educators in schools. The **American Orff-Schulwerk Association** is an organization dedicated specifically to preserving the Orff-Schulwerk approach to music education.

Attending Clinics and Conventions

As a music educator, it is highly beneficial to attend clinics and conventions as resources for music education. **Conventions** offer ample opportunities to network with fellow music educators, which result in the exchange of teaching ideas, programs, and other helpful pedagogical ideas. **Networking** also allows the music educator the chance to collaborate with other colleagues, opening the door for inviting guest artists to the music program. Networking can also provide the music educator with chances to find a mentor or to become a mentor to an aspiring teacher. **Clinics** offer a multitude of benefits to both the music educator and to the participating ensemble. Clinics offer a way for ensembles to get an unbiased critique on a performance, while the music educator also gets professional feedback for an ensemble. Clinics allow both music educators and the ensemble to hear many other ensembles perform, giving the teacher and students a peer review of the quality and level of the students' performances.

Music Education Journals

The Journal of Research in Music Education is a major peer-reviewed research journal in the field of music education published by Sage Publications for the National Association for Music Education. *The Music Educators Journal* is another peer-reviewed journal published by Sage, featuring scholarly and practical articles on music teaching. *The International Journal of Music Education* is a scholarly peer-reviewed journal published quarterly by Sage as part of the International Society of Music Education. *The Bulletin of the Council for Research in Music Education* is an academic journal covering peer-reviewed original research in the field of music education that is published quarterly by the University of Illinois Press for the Council for Research in Music Education. *The Journal of Band Research* features scholarly articles on band music, history, and methodology, and is the official publication of the American Bandmasters Association.

Administrative Duties

The responsibilities of a music educator include more than just designing and implementing a music curriculum; they also include the **logistical aspects** of running a music program. Music educators must be able to balance the **budget** allotted for the music program through the school. This involves buying and maintaining the appropriate number of instruments and music materials needed for the students without exceeding allotted program funds. Accurate and thorough bookkeeping combined with a strategic view of inventory maintenance will help a music educator maintain a healthy budget. Music educators must **log inventory** and keep track of all materials and instruments. Administrative duties also include **scheduling** student rehearsals, practices, lessons, contests, conferences, and performances. Music educators can use scheduling programs for better organization and delegate students' own scheduling. Contests, conferences, and performances should be planned well ahead of a season's start date so that educators can plan promotional materials, marketing, and performance curriculum.

Minimizing Financial Cost of a Music Program

Music programs in the current decade face many financial challenges within school districts; when faced with budget cuts, music programs must find ways to minimize the financial impact of their annual operating costs. **Loaning** music from other programs or libraries can reduce spending on new scores and music. Some movie theaters screen performances of operas, symphonies, and other concerts at a lower cost than a live theater performance. Consider distributing course materials electronically when possible, as printing costs that may seem small in isolation will accumulate over the course of a year. In a program that provides instruments that will be shared among students, ensure regular **maintenance** and instrument care to prevent damage that could mean expensive repair or replacements. A director should attempt to design performances and outreach efforts in a way that will create value for the community, while creating political and financial support for the school.

Factors Affecting Student Participation in a School Music Program

Outcomes in a student's musical education are the result of complex interactions between a large number of variables, both genetic and environmental. The strongest factors impeding positive outcomes are those associated with **poverty**. Hunger, physical and emotional abuse, and chronic illness can lead to poor school performance, and health-risk behaviors are consistently linked with poor grades and test scores and lower educational attainment. **School health programs** have been shown to reduce health-risk behaviors and have a positive effect on academic achievement. **Supportive teacher-student relationships** have also been shown to positively affect social and academic outcomes for students, enabling them to feel secure in the learning environment. Students in high-poverty urban schools may benefit even more than their high-income counterparts from positive teacher-student relationships.

Major Contributions to Music Education

Dalcroze Method

The Dalcroze method was developed around 1900 by Swiss composer, musician, and pedagogue Émile Jaques-Dalcroze, who developed a system of music education through movement called **eurhythmics**, in which students use a kinesthetic approach to experience musical concepts. In the **Dalcroze method**, the body is seen as the instrument, and students discover expression, musicality, tempo, dynamics, style, and phrase structure through physical dialogue with the music. Without the ability to physically respond to music, Dalcroze believed that no human could be fully musical. The approach uses eurhythmics, solfege, and improvisation to facilitate musical development in children. In a typical **eurhythmics class**, students will incorporate movement of their feet, arms, and bodies to music that is either improvised by the teacher or played from a recording. This method was brought to the United States in the early 1900s and slowly found its way into mainstream primary-level music education.

Kodály Method

The Kodály method was introduced in the 1950s by Hungarian composer, musician, ethnomusicologist, and educator Zoltán Kodály (1882–1967), who believed that music is an **innate part** of every human's experience and that **musical literacy** should be an integral part of every child's education. For Kodály, the main goal of musical education is singing; since music belongs to every human, and every culture has folk songs, the voice is then the most accessible instrument. To facilitate musical literacy for the masses, Kodály advocated the use of the movable-do system, hand signs for solfege syllables, rhythmic syllables, and solfa notation. The use of hand signs provides both a visual and kinesthetic tool for children so that the musical elements of pitch and intervals are first experienced and then identified. The **Kodály method** uses a five-step instructional sequence: Preparation, Make Conscious, Reinforcement, Practice, and Create, and it is foundational in early music education philosophies today.

Orff-Schulwerk Method

The Orff-Schulwerk method was developed in the 1920s by German composer, musician, and educator Carl Orff (1895–1982) and his close collaborator Gunild Keetman (1904–1990), who believed that music should be **actively experienced** and is best learned through a child's natural tendency to play. In the **Orff approach**, students explore music through the integration of drama, speech, and movement. Students are encouraged to play an active part in their musical development through improvisation on pitched and unpitched musical instruments. The **Orff-Schulwerk method** emphasizes rhythm development through chanting and bodily rhythm patterns and movement, and melodic development through improvisation of speaking patterns and specialized Orff instruments. The **pentatonic scale** is the most common scale used in the method, as it is most accessible on the Orff instruments. The Orff-Schulwerk approach is common in today's elementary music classrooms and is found in schools around the world.

Suzuki Method

The Suzuki method was developed in the mid-20th century by Japanese violinist, educator, and composer Shinichi Suzuki (1898–1998), who believed that musical development is best structured through a **mother tongue** approach, where children hear and learn to play music from an early age, as with speech. The **Suzuki method** emphasizes substantial parent involvement, an early start, listening, and repetition, similar to a child's language development. Creating an encouraging environment immensely helps a child's musical development. Students typically begin learning music by ear, and after developing competence on an instrument, learn to read music notation. The **Suzuki learning sequence** follows the language learning sequence, since children learn how to speak before they learn how to read. The Suzuki method offers a sequential repertoire for musical development on a variety of instruments and is found in many schools through use of the Suzuki repertoire, memorization of pieces, repetition, learning by rote, and continual parental involvement.

Bloom's Taxonomy of Learning as Related to Music Education

Bloom's taxonomy refers to the framework for educational goals and objectives for learning as laid out in the 1950s by Benjamin Bloom (1913–1999) and other educational psychologists. The model outlines hierarchical levels of thinking in three different domains: cognitive, affective, and psychomotor. Objectives for the **cognitive** domain focus on knowledge; for the **affective** domain, objectives focus on values; and for the **psychomotor**, objectives focus on physical motor skills. The model for the cognitive domain is most commonly referred to in music education as an assessment tool in forming and evaluating educational goals. The hierarchal levels in order are knowledge, comprehension, application, analysis, synthesis, and evaluation. In the **knowledge stage**, students must remember or recall information. In the **comprehension stage**, students must understand and be able to explain ideas and concepts. In the **application stage**, students apply the information in a new way. In the **analysis stage**, students must distinguish between different parts of the concept. In the **synthesis stage**, students must be able to gather the knowledge acquired to support and justify a decision. In the **evaluation stage**, students become independent to create and improvise original ideas.

Review Video: Bloom's Taxonomy
Visit mometrix.com/academy and enter code: 755020

Music Philosophy of Bennett Reimer

Bennett Reimer (1932–2013) was a prominent music educator and philosopher whose influential book, *A Philosophy of Music Education* (1970), promoted an **aesthetic model** of music education. For Reimer, music exists as an **expressive form**, and cannot be limited to intellectual or other non-musical pursuits. Its merit is in connecting people to feelings, and Reimer believed that because music is essentially dynamic sound waves, it is the only art form that can kindle mental feelings. Reimer argued for the **integration** of music in general education for the overall betterment of society's compassion and empathy. The best form of music education involves listening, examining, and actively participating in only musical works, which Reimer believed ought to be expressive. In a music curriculum, performance should not be the focus, since performance itself does not encourage active listening and the development of aesthetic feeling.

Laban's Theory of Movement Education

Rudolf von Laban (1879–1958) was a Hungarian dancer and theorist whose foundational movement theories for dance have been adopted by music educators for movement-based music education. Laban believed that all people should learn the **four elements of movement** to develop mindfulness and creativity. These four elements, or "effort" elements, are flow, weight, time, and space. **Flow** refers to free and tense movements; **weight** refers to heavy and light movements; **time** refers to quick and slow movements; and **space** refers to direct/straight and indirect/arcing movement. Laban also outlined eight basic actions: punch, slash, dab, flick, press, wring, glide, and float. Although these movement theories were originally intended for dance education, music educators have used these ideas to develop curriculum that incorporates effort elements and actions to express and interpret music, as well as in performance. These movements have also been adopted by conductors to convey musical gesture.

Music Philosophy of David Elliott

David Elliott (b. 1948) is a music educator and philosopher whose book, *Music Matters: A New Philosophy of Music Education* (1995), presents the **praxial philosophy** of music education, a direct departure from Reimer's aesthetic philosophy of music education. Elliott endorses a practical, procedural approach to music education, one that puts emphasis on the activity of, rather than the feeling that comes from, music making. To Elliott, musical knowledge is not just about familiarity and appreciation of musical works, but is also about the direct, purposeful skill set involved in making music. Central to Elliott's praxial philosophy is the concept of **musicianship**, a concept that encompasses both music making and music listening. Curriculum should be based on music practice and should start with music making even before students can fully comprehend the art of music making when listening to music. Elliott recommends a **student apprenticeship** model of education where the teacher plays the role of mentor and expert musician.

Career Opportunities in Music

Military Performance Opportunities for Musicians

The military offers a wealth of opportunities for the musician. The Army, Navy, Air Force, and Coast Guard all have full-time music ensembles. **Ensembles** are characterized as either Premier bands or Regional bands. The 10 **Premier bands** are based in Washington, D.C., or are attached to the academy of the relevant branch. Premier band ensemble members have a guaranteed post, without the potential for transfer to other locations. **Regional bands** are housed on bases domestically and abroad. Each "band" represents several different performing ensembles. The US Air Force Band, for example, oversees six entities: The Concert Band, Singing Sergeants (chorus), Airmen of Note (jazz ensemble), Air Force Strings, Ceremonial Brass, and Max Impact (rock). Military music careers are some of the most secure jobs in music, and provide extensive opportunities to tour, record, and perform at high-profile ceremonies, as well as college repayment, health care, and other benefits. Downsides relate to the fact that musicians are still military personnel and subject to the same disciplinary, bureaucratic, and legally binding service requirements as other military personnel.

Classical Performance vs. Popular Music Performance Career Opportunities

Career opportunities for musicians in classical performance parallel certain career opportunities for musicians in popular music performance. Both types of musicians can hold permanent or semi-permanent posts in performing ensembles, take contract gigs, give one-time performances, and hold teaching positions. Many **classical instrumentalists** can find jobs with regional symphony orchestras, concert bands, and opera orchestras, while **popular music instrumentalists** can find jobs with theaters, house bands, jazz orchestras, and studios. **Classical vocalists** can find jobs with symphony choruses, opera companies, and vocal ensembles. **Popular vocalists** can find jobs with studios, house bands, and jazz groups. Musicians in both classical and popular performance have union resources that support their members. Career opportunities for classical and popular musicians may differ in **demand**, as the current musical trend favors the popular musician who can contribute to studio productions, whereas the traditional symphonies, operas, and orchestras struggle with general public interest.

Aspiring Student Musicians

For aspiring student musicians, there are a multitude of performance opportunities and venues in which to hone their craft. Serious music students who want a deeper music experience may attend a **summer music program**. Performing art camps provide in-depth lessons, performance opportunities, and practice time, as well as traditional camp activities for social recreation. There are also summer programs on college campuses, which give students a glimpse into life at an undergraduate music college. Other summer programs may be instrument- or genre-specific, such as a jazz summer camp or a summer program for vocalists only. Some summer programs are offered in conjunction with a **music festival**, in which students immerse themselves in community performances and attend a showcase music festival as well. During the school year, students may audition or compete in local, regional, and national **competitions** that provide selected contestants with performance opportunities and publicity. Students can also seek out coffee houses that occasionally showcase student musicians.

Music Scholarships

The United States Marine Band, "President's Own," offers a concerto competition to high school woodwind, brass, and percussion students. Winners of the Marine Band Concerto Competition are awarded a performance as guest soloist with the United States Marine Band and a cash prize. The Williams Chorale Bacardi Fallon Scholarship Competition offers cash prizes and a performance opportunity to the top contestants of the competition. The Davidson Fellowship offers awards for original student compositions. The VSA Arts International Young Soloists Program gives monetary awards and performances in Washington, D.C., to students with disabilities. The Tri-M Music Honor Society Chapter of the Year Music Scholarships award top student chapters the opportunity for summer music study. The Glenn Miller Birthplace Society Scholarship gives high school winners the chance to perform at the Glenn Miller Festival.

Preparatory Education and Training

Careers in Music Business

Music business covers the legal, financial, ethical, and artistic aspects of managing a music business. For a career in music business, many students undertake an **undergraduate degree** in music business, finishing with a B.A. in Music Business. Some students may continue higher education, achieving an **MBA** in Music Business as well. A degree will help to qualify a student in music business, but it is just as important to get **hands-on training** through an internship and a foot in the door for the highest likelihood of success in the industry. Jobs within music business include artist manager, booking agent, business manager, recording studio owner, music publisher, Internet marketing specialist, media promotion specialist, concert or event promoter, arts and entertainment writer, publicist, product manager, recording studio manager, artist and repertoire scout, account executive, finance assistant, artist liaison, tour manager, booking agent, independent radio promoter, and music licensing supervisor.

Careers in Music Education

A career in music education offers musicians the option to teach a wide variety of subjects, from general music classes to orchestra, band, and choir, as well as subjects like music theory and music history in a public, private, or parochial school. Music educators should hold a minimum of a **bachelor's degree** in music education, along with the proper state teaching certifications. Educators whose goal is to teach in secondary education should **specialize** in the appropriate area, whether orchestra, band, or choir. Music educators whose goal is to teach in college, conservatory, or university settings should aim for a doctorate or terminal degree in music to be considered for most tenured professorships. There are opportunities to teach in a community college with only a Master's degree, but an applicant will be more competitive with a doctorate or terminal degree.

Job Opportunities Within Music Technology

There are various job opportunities within the field of music technology, as it has many specialized occupations that are constantly growing and changing. **Audio equipment technicians** oversee the audio and visual equipment for venues as diverse as concert halls, theaters, theme parks, and sporting events. Audio equipment technicians ensure the correct wiring and placement of microphones, soundboards, video screens, projectors, cables, and speakers. **Sound engineers** produce and edit sound effects, files, and other media for theater productions, art venues, and other entertainment scenes. **Recording engineers** operate sound recording equipment and help in mixing and editing the resulting files for production. Music technology careers also include Internet publishing, multimedia production, music software design, music hardware design, CD audio production, sound design, computer-based education and training, and music publishing.

Music Therapy

The undergraduate music therapy curriculum contains coursework encompassing a thorough study of music; psychology; the biological, social, and behavioral sciences; and disabilities, in addition to general studies. Through required fieldwork, **music therapy** students learn to assess client needs, develop and implement treatment plans, and evaluate and document clinical changes. Strong communication and interpersonal skills are absolutely mandatory in order to establish caring and professional relationships with people of all ages and abilities. Successful music therapists will be empathetic, creative, and open-minded, in order to better understand patients and themselves. Students considering a career in music therapy should look to gain experience in **allied health** through volunteer opportunities or summer work in nursing homes, camps for children with disabilities, and other settings where they can learn to serve the needs of people with disabilities.

Performing Arts Medicine

Performing arts medicine includes all disciplines that oversee and promote the health of the performing artist. Career opportunities can include medical professionals, artist educators, and administrators who strive to advocate the health of performing artists. Medical health professionals evaluate and treat any medical problems that may occur in dancers, singers, instrumentalists, and actors at all stages of their careers. The medical health professional may suggest physical therapy, occupational therapy, speech therapy, psychological services, or other forms of arts-specific rehabilitation. The focus of many **performing arts medical professionals** is to prevent re-injury, but the treatment may also cover technique, repertoire, instrument state, and emotional state adjustments as related to the injury. Career opportunities are also present in the continuing education and advocacy for injury prevention and healthy habits for the performing artist.

Physically Healthy Performance Practices

Long Exposure over Time to High dB

As a musician, it is extremely important to be aware of the risks of long exposure over time to **high dB listening experiences**, as high dB listening experiences occur almost daily for some musicians through band practice and rock concerts. When the **inner ear** is exposed to high dB sound over time, irreversible damage can occur in the nerve fibers and structures of the inner ear. Since damage that occurs over time is a **gradual process**, a musician may not be aware of hearing loss until it has already occurred. Symptoms include distorted or muffled hearing, difficulty hearing high-pitched sounds such as doorbells, bird chirps, and alarm clocks, pain or ringing in the ear after exposure to excessively loud sounds, and trouble understanding group conversations or conversations on the phone.

Measures to Protect Their Hearing

The ear and its hearing mechanisms provide a unique and essential role for the musician; deliberate measures should be taken to protect hearing and avoid permanent damage that can occur over time when exposed to high dB listening experiences. Musicians should **limit** band practices to two hours, as the average sound intensity of a band practice is 90 decibels, a potentially hazardous level of sound if experienced frequently over long periods of time. If musicians must practice at high sound levels frequently or for a long period of time, proper **hearing protection** should be used, such as earplugs and earmuffs. Musicians should also avoid listening to music on portable music devices at high volume levels, or levels above 85 decibels, for a long period of time. Damage that occurs to the inner ear cannot be medically or surgically corrected and constitutes permanent hearing loss.

Issues in Vocal Health

Vocal health should be a central priority for singers and non-singers alike. As a unique organ and instrument, the **voice** plays an essential role in daily communication as well as in music making. An unhealthy voice can become raspy, hoarse, strained, or raw, presenting difficulty in singing and in speech. **Proper hydration** should be maintained to clear the mucus and moisturize the throat. Find alternatives to yelling, such as clapping, ringing a bell, or moving closer to the person. Reduce background noise so that the voice does not need to be raised. Make sure to get proper **rest** for both the vocal mechanisms and the body through ample sleep time. Avoid drinking excessive alcohol, smoking, and inhaling chemical fumes that dehydrate and can damage the lungs. Be sure not to sing loudly on any high pitch that feels strained or uncontrolled.

Selecting Appropriate Repertoire

Appropriate Jazz Standards

For a beginning jazz band, a director should choose repertoire based on the opportunity it presents to play and experiment in the new idiom, taking advantage of the unique aspects of jazz music in a way that is educational and engaging. These features may include focusing on swing feeling, sectional solos, and other harmonic and structural features. **Charts** should provide the opportunity for students to take improvised solos, and students on all instruments, including the rhythm section, should be encouraged to experiment with improvisation. Popular publishers with charts for beginning jazz bands include Hal Leonard, Alfred, and Kendor. These arrangements are tailored to beginning musicians and may include **sample solos** that can be used as teaching tools. The director may wish to consider jazz standards with common chord changes such as "I've Got Rhythm" or a simple 12-bar blues. Over the course of the school year, the director may want to find charts that will allow different soloists to play featured parts.

Identifying Suitable Tunes for Beginning Jazz Improviser

Once the basics of improvisation have been established, the next step is to apply that learning in the context of a full song. This song will likely follow the standard head/solos/head structure. Full tunes for the **beginning improviser** should have characteristics that allow a student to focus attention on a limited number of variables at one time. Songs should have a moderate tempo, a strong tonal center, and preferably no more than three or four different chords. These characteristics will allow the student time to play within each chord, focus on only the notes that are "strong" within the different chords of the song, and appreciate the sound of the same notes in different chordal contexts. The goal in introducing improvisation within this context is to reduce the number of choices of what note to play, a common **hurdle** for the beginning improviser, and direct the student's **focus** to playing with confidence, remaining oriented within the song while improvising, and other aspects of performance (rhythm, dynamics, space) that eventually lead to more varied and interesting improvisations.

Performance Competencies for Students in Pre-K

Students in Pre-K should experience music as much as possible through listening, feeling, moving, and experimenting with their own vocal pitch and timbre. Children in this age range should be encouraged to freely use their voices in singing, chanting, and speaking along with music accompaniment and on their own. Students in Pre-K should experience a wide range of instrumental sounds and improvise their own melodies and patterns on different instruments. Students should practice relating musical sounds to other objects, symbols, and animals that are familiar to them to engage their imagination and encourage creative responses. Students in Pre-K should become increasingly accurate in their pitch matching and rhythm matching through their voices or on instruments. Students should experience a wide variety of genres and styles as well as be able to identify basic differences and changes in music.

Physiology of Vocal Range Development

Until puberty, a child's vocal mechanisms are not fully developed and do not contain the full range of the adult voice. Infants are born with a very high **larynx**; the larynx drops slightly when a child reaches the age of three. From age three until about age 10–13, the larynx is not yet fully functional. The **vocal folds** of a child are much shorter than an adult's vocal folds, and the larynx of a child sits higher than an adult's. The vocal range of a child is relatively **limited** as compared to an adult; high and low pitches are reached by the lengthening or thickening of the vocal folds. During puberty, a child's larynx grows to its full size, drops, and the vocal cords lengthen and thicken substantially. The fully matured vocal mechanisms acquire a vocal range much larger than a child's, functioning through the complex muscular and cartilage actions within the larynx to produce wide-ranging pitches in different registers.

Transposition and Instrumental Ranges

Woodwind Instruments

Woodwind instruments include single reeds, double reeds, and flutes. All woodwind instruments have side holes that are left open or covered to change the sounding length of the tube. The **piccolo** is typically notated on the treble clef an octave higher and has a general range of D4-C7. The **flute** is typically notated on the treble clef with no transposition, and has a general range of Bb3-D7. The **oboe** is typically notated on the treble clef with no transposition and has a general range of Bb3-A6. The **clarinet** is typically notated on the treble clef with the Bb clarinet sounding a major second lower, the A clarinet sounding a minor third lower, the D clarinet sounding a major second higher, the Eb clarinet sounding a minor third higher, and all with a general range of E3-C7. The **bassoon** is typically notated on the bass or tenor clefs with no transposition and has a general range of Bb1-Eb5.

Brass Instruments

Brass instruments include those wind instruments that are typically made with metal and sounded by the vibration of the player's lips through a mouthpiece. The **French horn** is typically notated on the treble or bass clefs sounded a perfect fifth lower with a general range of F#2-C6. The **trumpet** is typically notated on the treble clef with the C trumpet sounding as written and the Bb trumpet sounding a major second lower, both with a general range of F#3-D6. The **tenor trombone** is typically notated on the bass, tenor, or alto clefs sounding as written, with a general range of E2-F5. The **bass trombone** is typically notated on the bass clef sounding as written, with a general range of Bb1-Bb4. The **tuba** is typically notated on the bass clef sounding as written, with a general range of G0-C5. The **euphonium** is typically notated on the bass or treble clefs sounding as written on the bass clef or a major ninth lower on the treble clef, with a general range of Bb1-F5.

String Instruments

String instruments include those instruments whose main vibrating system is a string set into motion by plucking, striking, or bowing. The **violin** is typically notated in the treble clef sounding as written, with a general range of G3-A7. The **viola** is typically notated in the alto clef sounding as written, with a general range of C3-E6. The **cello** is typically notated in the bass, tenor, and treble clefs sounding as written, with a general range of C2-C6. The **double bass** is typically notated in bass clef sounding an octave lower, with a general range of C2-C5. The **banjo** is typically notated in treble clef sounding as written, with a general range of C3-A4. The **guitar** is typically notated in treble clef sounding an octave lower, with a general range of E3-E6. The **harp** is typically notated on the grand staff sounding as written, with a general range of Cb1-G#7.

Percussion Instruments

Pitched percussion instruments can include membranophones as well as idiophones that have definite pitches. The **timpani** is typically notated in bass clef sounding as written with the 30-inch timpani in a range of D2-A2, the 28-inch timpani in a range of F2-C3, the 25-inch timpani in a range of Bb2-F3, and the 23-inch timpani in a range of D3-A3. The **xylophone** is typically notated in treble clef sounding an octave higher, with a general range of G4-C7. The **marimba** is typically notated on the grand staff sounding as written, with a general range of C2 or A2 to C7. The **glockenspiel** is typically notated in treble clef sounding two to eight octaves higher, with a general range of G3-C6. The **vibraphone** is typically notated in treble clef sounding as written, with a general range of F3-F6. **Chimes** are typically notated in treble clef sounding an octave higher, with a general range of C4-G5.

Keyboard Instruments

Keyboard instruments include those instruments whose sound-producing mechanisms are set into motion through a system of levers and keys. The **keyboard** is generally made up of seven natural and five chromatic keys. The distance between the natural keys are whole steps except for the half steps between E-F and B-C. The **modern piano** is typically notated on the grand staff sounding as written, with a general range of A0-C8. The **celesta** is typically notated on the grand staff sounding an octave higher, with a general range of C3-C7. The **harpsichord** is typically notated on the grand staff sounding as written, with a general range of F1-F6. The **harmonium** is typically notated on the grand staff sounding as written, with a general range of F1-F6. The **organ** is typically notated on the grand staff sounding as written, with a general range of C2-C7.

Selecting Music Selections for an Advanced High School Ensemble

As a music educator, it is important to select appropriately leveled, culturally diverse music selections to reflect the musical diversity within the global community as well as to challenge the students in a variety of styles and genres. Music directors should select a **variety** of music that is below, at, and above an ensemble's level to provide opportunities for in-depth expressive growth without technical obstacles, as well as music that challenges the students technically to reach the next level. Music directors can consult **state contest repertoire** lists for a general list of appropriate repertoire, as well as published repertoire books. Culturally diverse composers such as Soon Hee Newbold, William Grant Still, Dorothy Rudd Moore, and Yasuhide Ito offer many works that would be appropriate for an advanced high school ensemble.

Devising a Core Repertoire List for an Ensemble

When devising a core repertoire list for an ensemble, it is important to take many musical aspects into consideration. A **core repertoire list** should provide a strong framework of music education for the students, factoring in the students' musical growth and development. A core repertoire list should include a variety of rhythmic features that challenge the ensemble's **technical abilities**. The harmonic language of the repertoire list should be varied and span a wide range of genres. The melodic lines within the repertoire should exhibit creative writing and expressive interest for the students. The repertoire should also be well orchestrated, providing musical interest in all sections of the ensemble, as well as providing a balance between tutti and thinner textures. The repertoire should provide some works that are deeply expressive, to allow students to expand their musical expressive language. The core repertoire list should be well sequenced in introducing new musical concepts as well reinforcing old ones.

Repertoire Sources

Choral directors should choose intermediate middle school choir repertoire that is of high quality, teachable, and appropriate for the range, ability level, cultural context, and programming considerations of the ensemble. There are many repertoire sources for the middle school choral director that can assist in preliminary repertoire selections. The **American Choral Directors Association** publishes multiple repertoire lists including "Tried and True Literature" for junior high choirs, as well as annual honor choir repertoire lists. Donald Roach's *Complete Secondary Choral Music Guide* includes extensive repertoire lists, music theater sources, and other content that is valuable for the middle school choral director. Music directors can also consult **state clinic and**

contest repertoire lists. Several publishing companies also produce suggested repertoire for intermediate choirs as well as complete compilations of choral works for the middle school choir.

Using Colleagues, Mentors, Conferences, and Publishers as Repertoire Resources

A conscientious director should be willing to look to a diverse variety of sources for repertoire. By drawing from colleagues, mentors, conferences, and publishers, the director can tap the experience of people of different tastes, ages, backgrounds, and musical circles. Suggestions from those with a **different approach** to choosing repertoire can be particularly valuable, as these suggestions are the most likely to be overlooked by a search undertaken independently. **Publishers** may be useful due to their access not only to their own catalogs, including back catalog that may have been previously overlooked, but also to the catalogs in the publisher's extended network. As publishing houses have consolidated and collections have become digitized, repertoire that may have only been available from small boutique publishers has become available for wider circulation.

Common Pedagogical Approaches

Phyllis Weikart

Phyllis Weikart (1931–2016) wrote numerous books on the pedagogical applications of music and movement and is the author of *Movement Plus Music* (a music education guide for learning through movement for ages 3–7), *Round the Circle: Key Experiences in Movement*, and *Teaching Movement and Dance: A Sequential Approach to Rhythmic Movement*, among others. She served on the faculty of the Division of Kinesiology at the University of Michigan and was also the founder of the program **Education Through Movement: Building the Foundation**, a research-based approach to learning through movement and music. In the **Weikart method**, kinesthetic experiences are broken down into individual units. First, the movements must be isolated and modeled to the students, then the movement may be simplified and built upon, and finally, the students must have a variety of opportunities to use the movements in personal and creative ways. Through her program, Weikart provides a detailed, sequential approach to movement-based musical tasks, and continues the traditions developed by Dalcroze and Orff-Schulwerk.

Comprehensive Musicianship through Performance

The Comprehensive Musicianship through Performance initiative is a model that prioritizes an inclusive, deeper understanding of music for lifelong musical involvement, rather than a narrow-minded exclusive learning model. In the model, the rehearsal becomes a **learning laboratory**, with the teacher acting as a musical facilitator rather than merely as a lecturer or conductor. The chosen musical selection becomes a vessel for **musical discovery**; as students prepare the selection, the instructor provides a holistic approach for different objectives and different learning styles. The model encompasses a wide possibility of student outcomes, from knowledge of music history, style, and composition, to form, structure, and theory. The five main elements of the CMP educational process are music selection, objectives, analysis, strategies, and assessment. These segments may be used in any order to plan a music curriculum. **Analysis** involves a deeper understanding of the history, form, and style of a musical selection. The educator then decides on the learning **objectives** through **musical selection**. **Strategies** for musical discovery and performance are implemented in the curriculum, and the educator **assesses** students' needs and educational outcomes.

Review Video: Learning Objectives
Visit mometrix.com/academy and enter code: 528458

Gordon's Music Learning Theory and Audiation

Edwin Gordon (1927–2015) developed the Music Learning Theory in the 1950s to describe how students learn music and how it should be taught. The theory centers on the concept of **audiation**, a term Gordon uses to describe the internalization of music when performing, listening, or composing. Gordon differentiates audiation from aural perception, as aural perception is an involuntary response to sound in the brain, whereas audiation requires cognitive processing in the brain to give meaning to the sound. Gordon delineates eight different types of audiation. **Type 1** involves listening to familiar or unfamiliar music; **Type 2** involves reading familiar or unfamiliar music; **Type 3** encompasses writing familiar or unfamiliar music via dictation; **Type 4** involves recalling and performing familiar music from memory; **Type 5** deals with recalling and writing familiar music from memory; **Type 6** involves creating and improvising unfamiliar music; **Type 7** involves creating and improvising unfamiliar music while reading; and **Type 8** deals with creating and improvising unfamiliar music while writing.

Orff-Schulwerk Lesson Plan

The Orff-Schulwerk approach to music education, developed in the 1920s, emphasizes children's natural tendency to play as a key component to musical discovery and development. Students are given the opportunity to explore various rhythms, melodies, and songs, and then imitate, improvise, and create their own rhythms, melodies, and songs. Central activity components of an Orff-Schulwerk lesson include speech, singing, movement, and playing instruments. The Orff approach holds that musical development begins with a child's **natural speech**; children use common chants and rhymes to explore rhythmic stress patterns. Along with speech, the Orff method uses **singing** to introduce tonal patterns and strengthen children's singing abilities. Singing activities are most commonly formatted as **games** and simple songs to encourage students' natural tendency to play. Movement through games is also an important activity component, as music and movement are fundamentally intertwined in the Orff-Schulwerk philosophy. The model Orff-Schulwerk activity is the use of instruments; common instruments include body percussion, hand instruments, and specialized Orff instruments built specifically to facilitate easy access for children. These include the bass, alto, soprano xylophones and metallophones, and the soprano and alto glockenspiel.

Dalcroze Eurhythmics

The Dalcroze approach to music education, developed in the early 20th century, makes use of physical movement as a tool for musical development. Émile Jacques-Dalcroze believed that music should be taught with **kinesthetic movement** so that sound can be integrated with nerves and muscles, and articulated through bodily motion. Dalcroze theorized that music can be more readily understood through movement than reason, and musical education should start with movement before intellectual concepts can be introduced. In this framework, the body is the instrument, and students discover expression, musicality, tempo, dynamics, style, and phrase structure through inner dialogue with the music. In this way, students develop musicality with a deeper understanding of their physical connection to music and refine their senses of rhythm, coordination, hearing, and creativity.

Pre-K Eurhythmics

Sample activities for a Pre-K eurhythmics class can include:

- Students dance freely to a teacher's improvisation on the piano, with the improvisation frequently changing in relation to mood, tempo, dynamics, and style. Students must change their dance styles accordingly.
- Students must pass a beach ball around in a circle in rhythm, as defined by the teacher's music.

- Students stomp their feet in rhythm and sway side to side while the teacher recites a children's rhyme.
- Students clap their hands to the tempo of the teacher's improvisation at the piano; the teacher alters the tempo of the music so that students must follow along.

The teacher plays a soft melody on the piano while the students move smoothly to the music; for every sudden sforzando chord played, students must clap hands with a partner, then resume the quiet music/movement.

Chapter Quiz

Ready to see how well you retained what you just read? Scan the QR code to go directly to the chapter quiz interface for this study guide. If you're using a computer, simply visit the online resources page at **mometrix.com/resources719/nesincmusic** and click the Chapter Quizzes link.

Integration of Knowledge and Understanding

Preparing for an Essay Question

Brainstorm

Spend the first three to five minutes brainstorming for ideas. Write down any ideas that you might have on the topic. The purpose is to pull any helpful information from the depths of your memory. In this stage, anything goes down in a margin for notes regardless of how good or bad the idea may seem at first glance.

Strength Through Different Viewpoints

The best papers will contain several examples and mature reasoning. As you brainstorm, you should consider different perspectives. There are more than two sides to every topic. In an argument, there are countless perspectives that can be considered. On any topic, different groups are impacted and many reach the same conclusion or position. Yet, they reach the same conclusion through different paths. Before writing your essay, try to *see* the topic through as many different *eyes* as you can.

In addition, you don't have to use information on how the topic impacts others. You can draw from your own experience as you wish. If you prefer to use a personal narrative, then explain the experience and your emotions from that moment. Anything that you've seen in your community can be expanded upon to round out your position on the topic.

Once you have finished with your creative flow, you need to stop and review what you brainstormed. *Which idea allowed you to come up with the most supporting information?* Be sure to pick an angle that will allow you to have a thorough coverage of the prompt.

Every garden of ideas has weeds. The ideas that you brainstormed are going to be random pieces of information of different values. Go through the pieces carefully and pick out the ones that are the best. The best ideas are strong points that will be easy to write a paragraph in response.

Now, you have your main ideas that you will focus on. So, align them in a sequence that will flow in a smooth, sensible path from point to point. With this approach, readers will go smoothly from one idea to the next in a reasonable order. Readers want an essay that has a sense of continuity (i.e., Point 1 to Point 2 to Point 3 and so on).

Start Your Engines

Now, you have a logical flow of the main ideas for the start of your essay. Begin by expanding on the first point, then move to your second point. Pace yourself. Don't spend too much time on any one of the ideas that you are expanding on. You want to have time for all of them. Make sure that you watch your time. If you have twenty minutes left to write out your ideas and you have four ideas, then you can only use five minutes per idea. Writing so much information in so little time can be an intimidating task. Yet, when you pace yourself, you can get through all of your points. If you find that you are falling behind, then you can remove one of your weaker arguments. This will allow you to give enough support to your remaining paragraphs.

Once you finish expanding on an idea, go back to your brainstorming session where you wrote out your ideas. You can scratch through the ideas as you write about them. This will let you see what you need to write about next and what you have left to cover.

Your introductory paragraph should have several easily identifiable features.

- First, the paragraph should have a quick description or paraphrasing of the topic. Use your own words to briefly explain what the topic is about.
- Second, you should list your writing points. What are the main ideas that you came up with earlier? If someone was to read only your introduction, they should be able to get a good summary of the entire paper.
- Third, you should explain your opinion of the topic and give an explanation for why you feel that way. What is your decision or conclusion on the topic?

Each of your following paragraphs should develop one of the points listed in the main paragraph. Use your personal experience and knowledge to support each of your points. Examples should back up everything.

Once you have finished expanding on each of your main points, you need to conclude your essay. Summarize what you have written in a conclusion paragraph. Explain once more your argument on the prompt and review why you feel that way in a few sentences. At this stage, you have already backed up your statements. So, there is no need to do that again. You just need to refresh your readers on the main points that you made in your essay.

Don't Panic

Whatever you do during essay, do not panic. When you panic, you will put fewer words on the page and your ideas will be weak. Therefore, panicking is not helpful. If your mind goes blank when you see the prompt, then you need to take a deep breath. Force yourself to go through the steps listed above: brainstorm and put anything on scratch paper that comes to mind.

Also, don't get clock fever. You may be overwhelmed when you're looking at a page that is mostly blank. Your mind is full of random thoughts and feeling confused, and the clock is ticking down faster. You have already brainstormed for ideas. Therefore, you don't have to keep coming up with ideas. If you're running out of time and you have a lot of ideas that you haven't written down, then don't be afraid to make some cuts. Start picking the best ideas that you have left and expand on them. Don't feel like you have to write on all of your ideas.

A short paper that is well written and well organized is better than a long paper that is poorly written and poorly organized. Don't keep writing about a subject just to add sentences and avoid repeating a statement or idea that you have explained already. The goal is 1 to 2 pages of quality writing. That is your target, but you should not mess up your paper by trying to get there. You want to have a natural end to your work without having to cut something short. If your essay is a little long, then that isn't a problem as long as your ideas are clear and flow well from paragraph to paragraph. Remember to expand on the ideas that you identified in the brainstorming session.

Leave time at the end (at least three minutes) to go back and check over your work. Reread and make sure that everything you've written makes sense and flows well. Clean up any spelling or grammar mistakes. Also, go ahead and erase any brainstorming ideas that you weren't able to include. Then, clean up any extra information that you might have written that doesn't fit into your paper.

As you proofread, make sure that there aren't any fragments or run-ons. Check for sentences that are too short or too long. If the sentence is too short, then look to see if you have a specific subject and an active verb. If it is too long, then break up the long sentence into two sentences. Watch out for any "big words" that you may have used. Be sure that you are using difficult words correctly. Don't misunderstand; you should try to increase your vocabulary and use difficult words in your essay. However, your focus should be on developing and expressing ideas in a clear and precise way.

The Short Overview

Depending on your preferences and personality, the essay may be your hardest or your easiest section. You are required to go through the entire process of writing a paper in a limited amount of time which is very challenging.

Stay focused on each of the steps for brainstorming. Go through the process of creative flow first. You can start by generating ideas about the prompt. Next, organize those ideas into a smooth flow. Then, pick out the ideas that are the best from your list.

Create a recognizable essay structure in your paper. Start with an introduction that explains what you have decided to argue. Then, choose your main points. Use the body paragraphs to touch on those main points and have a conclusion that wraps up the topic.

Save a few moments to go back and review what you have written. Clean up any minor mistakes that you might have made and make those last few critical touches that can make a huge difference. Finally, be proud and confident of what you have written!

NES Practice Test

Want to take this practice test in an online interactive format?
Check out the online resources page, which includes interactive practice questions and much more: **mometrix.com/resources719/nesincmusic**

1. Use the example below to answer the question that follows.

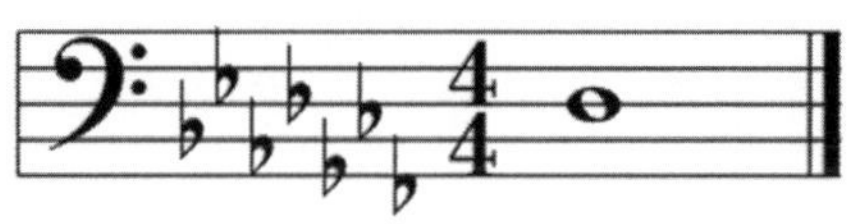

Which of the following is the name of the note in the above example?

a. B-flat
b. D
c. B
d. D-flat

2. Which of the following examples should be performed at an extremely slow and broad tempo?

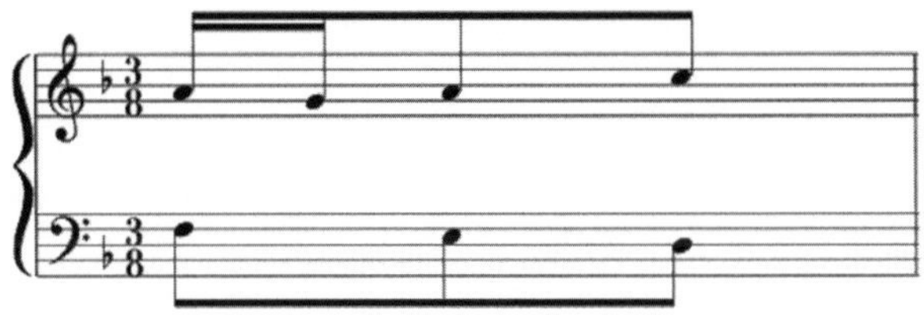

a. Andante

b. Larghissimo

c. Largo

d. Larghetto

3. Use the example below to answer the question that follows.

Which of the following is the articulation that indicates the note is to be played at full length or slightly longer?

a. Accent
b. Staccato
c. Tenuto
d. Fermata

4. Use the example below to answer the question that follows.

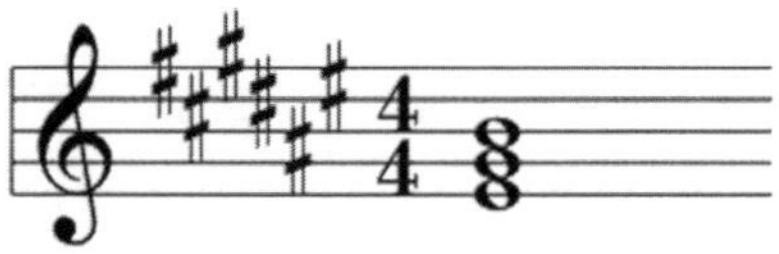

The chord in the above example can be best described as which of the following?

a. vii°
b. V
c. ii
d. iv

5. Use the example below to answer the question that follows.

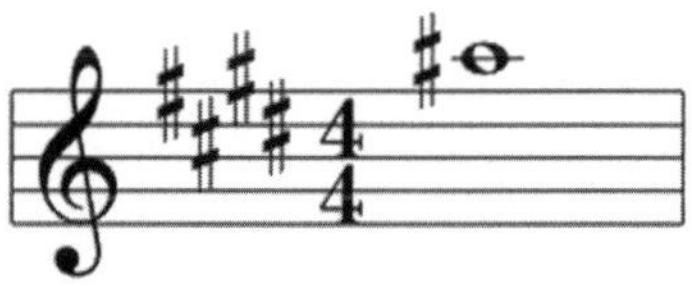

Which of the following is the name of the note in the above example?

a. C-sharp
b. E-sharp
c. A-sharp
d. G-sharp

6. Use the example below to answer the question that follows.

What is the implied time signature of the example above?

a. 3/4
b. 6/8
c. 12/4
d. 9/8

7. Use the example below to answer the question that follows.

Name the harmony in the above example.

a. C°7
b. Aø7
c. G °7
d. Eb ø7

8. Use the example below to answer the question that follows.

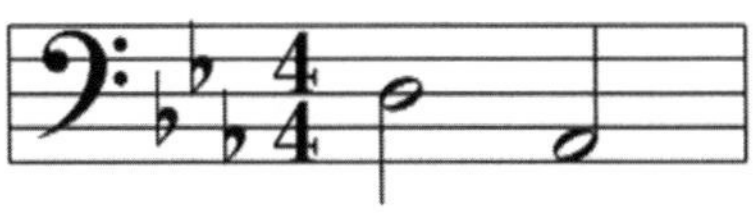

Which of the following best describes the melodic interval in the above example?

a. Perfect fourth
b. Diminished fifth
c. Augmented fourth
d. Major fifth

9. Use the example below to answer the question that follows.

Which of the following best describes the seventh chord in the above example?

a. Major seventh in third inversion
b. Dominant seventh in second inversion
c. Major/minor seventh in third inversion
d. Minor seventh in second inversion

10. Use the example below to answer the question that follows.

Which of the following chord progressions best describes the above example?

a. $\text{ii}^{6}/_{4}$ – V – vi^{6} - iii
b. I^{6} – IV – $\text{V}^{6}/_{4}$ - ii
c. IV – $\text{V}^{6}/_{4}$ – I - ii
d. iii^{6} – V – $\text{I}^{6}/_{4}$ - IV

11. Use the example below to answer the question that follows.

Which of the following best describes the above cadence?

a. Perfect authentic cadence
b. Plagal cadence
c. Deceptive cadence
d. Half cadence

12. Use the example below to answer the question that follows.

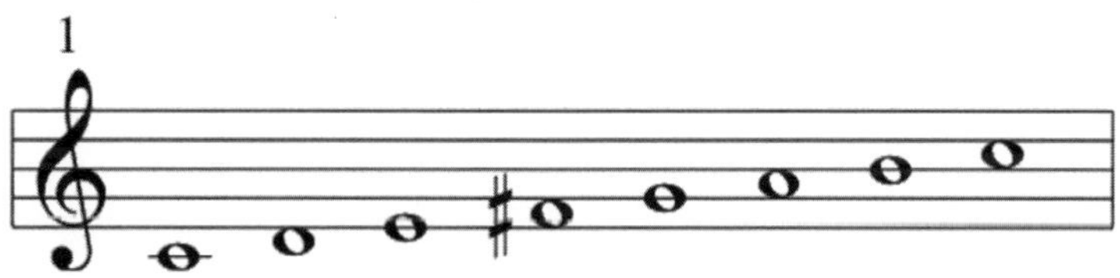

What is the musical mode shown in the example above?

a. Lydian
b. Dorian
c. Locrian
d. Phrygian

13. Use the example below to answer the question that follows.

Identify the type of dissonance found above the asterisk in the given voice-leading example.

a. Neighbor tone
b. Suspension
c. Passing tone
d. Appoggiatura

14. Use the example below to answer the question that follows.

Which of the following best describes the harmonic interval in the above example?

a. Augmented 7th
b. Minor 7th
c. Diminished 7th
d. Major 7th

15. Use the examples below to answer the following question.

Which of the following is a compound meter?

a. 

b. 

c. 

d. 

16. Use the example below to answer the question that follows.

The above excerpt is best subdivided into which pulse subdivisions?

a. 2-2-3
b. 5-2
c. 3-4
d. 3-2-2

17. Use the example below to answer the question that follows.

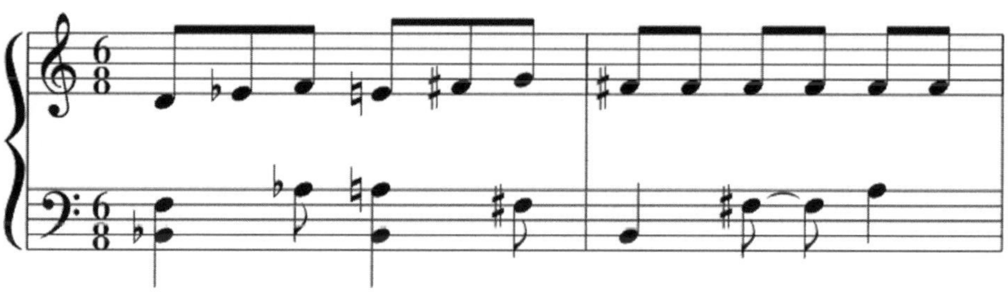

The second measure of the above example uses which rhythmic device?

a. Anacrusis
b. Horizontal hemiola
c. Suspension
d. Augmentation

18. Use the example below to answer the question that follows.

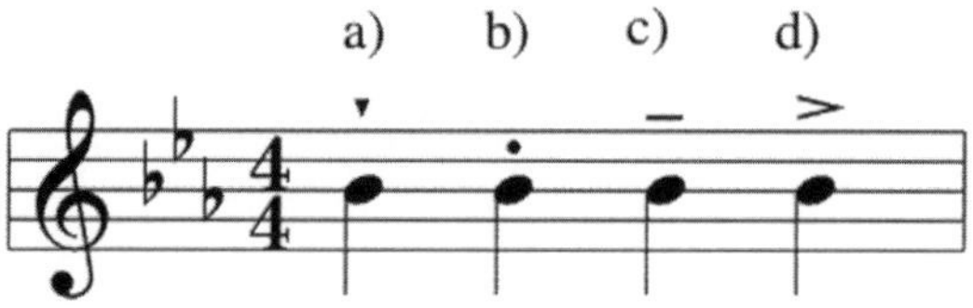

In the example, which articulation indicates that the note should be played with the shortest duration?

a. Staccatissimo
b. Staccato
c. Tenuto
d. Accent

19. The waltz form places rhythmic emphasis on which beat?

a. Second beat
b. All beats equally
c. Third beat
d. First beat

20. Which of the following musical terms comes from the Italian term meaning "to hurry"?

a. *Slentando*
b. *Allargando*
c. *Affrettando*
d. *Calando*

21. Use the example below to answer the question that follows.

The bass in the above example uses which of the following rhythmic patterns?

a. 3-2 clave
b. Ostinato
c. Bossa nova
d. Alberti bass

22. Which of the following typically describes rondo form?

a. AABBCC
b. ABBAB
c. ABACABA
d. AABA

23. Which of the following is NOT an example of compound musical form?

a. Sonata form
b. Binary form
c. Minuet and trio
d. Rondo form

24. The *ballade* refers to a musical form originally based on what literary form?

a. Play
b. Narrative
c. Soliloquy
d. Elegy

25. Which opera form of the Enlightenment featured three acts with alternating arias and recitatives with usually six or seven characters?

a. Opera buffa
b. Opera comique
c. Opera seria
d. Opera greco

26. Which of the following musical elements is a stylistic feature of the African musical tradition?

a. Dialogue
b. Modes
c. Discant
d. Coda

27. Which of the following compositional tools describes a group of closely spaced notes played simultaneously, usually in intervals of adjacent seconds and groupings?

a. Extended harmony
b. Tone cluster
c. Diminished seventh
d. Retrograde inversion

28. The jazz improvisational style can be most closely compared to what Classical musical style?

a. Baroque music
b. Minimalist music
c. Symphonic music
d. Impressionist music

29. Which of the following was an early form of polyphony during the Medieval period in which voices were sung in parallel motion?

a. Motet
b. Gregorian chant
c. Mass
d. Organum

30. Which movement of the 19th century featured music that evoked a place through the use of folk melodies?

a. Impressionism
b. Nationalism
c. Romanticism
d. Realism

31. The twelve-tone technique of music was created by:

a. Anton Webern
b. Milton Babbit
c. Arnold Schoenberg
d. Pierre Boulez

32. Which of the following is an example of *absolute music*, as opposed to *program music*?

a. *Symphony No. 5* by Ludwig van Beethoven
b. *Don Quixote* by Richard Strauss
c. *Danse Macabre* by Camille Saint-Saëns
d. *Symphonie Fantastique* by Hector Berlioz

33. Which period of classical Western music featured heavy ornamentation and improvised embellishment of a musical line?

a. Romantic
b. Baroque
c. 20th and 21st centuries
d. Classical

34. How did the orchestra shift the way it used certain instrument families from the Baroque to the Classical era?

a. Violins became the dominant string section, while the lower strings became the supporting background.
b. Strings and winds were doubled on every thematic line.
c. Bassoons became part of the supporting bass texture.
d. Woodwinds became the prominent rhythmic support section, while strings played secondary rhythmic roles.

35. Which of the following composers is most closely associated with music that featured brass with large orchestrations and increasingly powerful orchestral sounds?

a. Roger Sessions
b. Manuel de Falla
c. Béla Bartók
d. Igor Stravinsky

36. What is NOT a typical instrument of Appalachian folk music?

a. Dulcimer
b. Banjo
c. Tumbadora
d. Mandolin

37. Which American musical is considered by historians to be the first Broadway musical with a fully integrated, serious, continuous plot?

a. *Cats* by Andrew Lloyd Webber
b. *Show Boat* by Kern and Hammerstein
c. *Ain't Misbehavin'* by Horwitz and Maltby, Jr.
d. *Porgy and Bess* by George Gershwin

38. Which of the following is the earliest form of jazz music?

a. West Coast jazz
b. Kansas City blues
c. Latin jazz
d. New Orleans jazz

39. The Sugarhill Gang helped to widely popularize which term in their 1979 song *Rapper's Delight*?

a. Hip hop
b. Disco rap
c. Neo soul
d. Trip hop

40. The black church heavily influenced which of the following musical genres through improvisation, storytelling, and call and response?

a. Metal
b. Latin
c. Grunge
d. Blues

41. Cajun music of Louisiana traces its roots back to which European culture?

a. French
b. Dutch
c. Flemish
d. Portuguese

42. How does funk music differ from soul and R&B music?

a. Funk is based on an unconventional progression over many chords.
b. Funk is based on a melody line over whole-tone chords.
c. Funk is based on a rhythmic groove, bass lines, and simple chords.
d. Funk is based on the harmonic voice-leading of extended chords.

43. Of the following Cuban styles, which is derived from the mambo with a characteristic rhythmic pattern of two eighth notes followed by a quarter note?

a. Tresillo
b. Cha-cha-cha
c. Son montuno
d. Rumba

44. Call and response singing, polyrhythms, and improvised rhythms, are all common features of music from…

a. Africa.
b. Asia.
c. Europe.
d. North America.

45. Which of the following is a traditional form of Japanese theater that stems from the 1600s?

a. Kesho
b. Michiyuki
c. Shosagoto
d. Kabuki

46. The Middle Eastern *maqam* system of melodic organization is most similar to which aspect of Western music theory?

a. Counterpoint
b. Binary form
c. Modes
d. Notation

47. Ostinatos are found extensively in the music of which of the following countries?

a. China
b. Germany
c. Mexico
d. Ethiopia

48. Reggae music originated in which Caribbean nation in the 1960s?

a. Haiti
b. Cuba
c. Trinidad
d. Jamaica

49. Which of the following best expresses the role freedom songs played during the period of apartheid in South Africa?

a. They divided the oppressed and exposed the freedom of the government.
b. They calmed the oppressed and exposed the power of the government.
c. They united the oppressed and exposed the injustices of the government.
d. They defended the oppressed and exposed the loyalty of the government.

50. Which of the following is the purpose of a *leitmotif*?

a. It musically represents a person, place, or idea.
b. It musically protests a political uprising.
c. It musically records the historic events of a place.
d. It musically inspires the audience to do a specific action.

51. Composers typically use which of the following musical modes to convey sadness?

a. Major mode
b. Mixolydian mode
c. Minor mode
d. Lydian mode

52. A loud, forceful, and fast sound tends to convey which of the following moods?

a. Sorrow
b. Calm
c. Hope
d. Passion

53. Which major pedagogue developed the system of music education through movement called eurythmics?

a. Kodály
b. Dalcroze
c. Orff
d. Suzuki

54. When encountering a difficult passage, how do musicians most effectively practice that passage?

a. Playing it as fast as possible
b. Studying it away from the instrument
c. Playing it slowly and thoughtfully
d. Playing the sections before and after

55. Which of the following instrument groups would an orchestrator most likely choose to represent a lush canvas of passionate sound?

a. Percussion
b. Strings
c. Brass
d. Woodwinds

56. Which of the following articulations would best evoke a sense of raindrops?

a. Staccato
b. Legato
c. Tenuto
d. Fermata

57. Musical phrasing, contour, and line can be most analogous to:

a. The choice of subject and medium in a painting
b. The synchrony and interaction between dancers in a ballet
c. The melding of flavors and ingredients in culinary arts
d. The cadence and inflection of language in a narrated text

58. The Fibonacci sequence in mathematics can be seen in all of the following aspects of music EXCEPT:

a. The syncopation of dance forms with the golden ratio
b. Compositional climaxes of musical works at the golden ratio
c. Diatonic scales and the foundational structure of the tonic triad
d. The design and construction of instruments such as the violin

59. A performer's decision to add dramatic intent within a certain musical piece is conceptually most similar to:

a. A painter's decision to use white instead of black paint
b. An actor's personal interpretation of character lines
c. A writer's alternate ending of a novel
d. A dancer's warm-up before a debut performance

60. The structure of sonata form in music is most similar to which literary narrative structure?

a. Setup – bridge – resolution
b. Setup – plot – conflict
c. Setup – conflict – resolution
d. Setup – resolution – plot

61. The overtone series can be best understood within the context of which scientific discipline?

a. Chemistry
b. Biology
c. Physics
d. Astronomy

62. Which movement in music paralleled the movement in visual arts led by painters such as Monet, Cézanne, Degas, Manet, and Renoir?

a. Impressionism
b. Rococo
c. Neoclassicism
d. Abstraction

63. The rhythms of music are most related to:

a. The size of the canvas in a painting
b. The shape of a sculpture
c. The climax of the plot in a novel
d. The steps taken in dance

64. A career in music business would include which of the following job titles?

a. Composer
b. Publicist
c. Accompanist
d. Vocalist

65. Which of the following careers is concerned with overseeing and promoting the health of the performing artist?

a. Critical care medicine
b. Music therapy
c. Medical nutrition therapy
d. Performing arts medicine

66. Which of the following coursework would be most important to an aspiring audio engineer?

a. Recording technology
b. Music theory
c. Physics
d. Music business

67. What is the minimum education requirement for those wishing to enter a career in music education?

a. Associates in music education, with the proper state teaching certification
b. Doctor of musical arts in music education, with the proper state teaching certification
c. Bachelor's degree in music education, with the proper state teaching certification
d. Master's degree in music education, with the proper state teaching certification

68. What are the main incentives for aspiring performers to compete in local, regional, and national competitions?

a. High school and college admission
b. Performance opportunities and publicity
c. Financial and retirement stability
d. Music research and development

69. Of the following, which is the most secure job in music, providing extensive opportunities to tour, record, and perform at high-profile ceremonies as well as college repayment, health care, and other benefits?

a. Cruise ship musician
b. Orchestra musician
c. Military musician
d. Band musician

70. Which of the following would best help a music producer with career advancement in an increasingly competitive environment?

a. Increasing his or her social media output
b. Obtaining a master's degree in music
c. Buying the latest in audio technology
d. Diversifying his or her skill set

71. Which of the following forms is a monothematic composition in which a single subject is continually echoed throughout the piece through imitation and development?

a. Fugue form
b. Strophic form
c. Sectional variation
d. Rondo form

72. Which of the following should be done first when harmonizing a given melody?

a. Execution
b. Planning
c. Testing
d. Analysis

73. Which of the following is the most fundamental tool for beginning improvisation?

a. Syncopation
b. Imitation
c. Modulation
d. Inversion

74. What is the name of the motion of two musical lines where one line stays stationary while the other musical line moves in an upward or downward direction?

a. Contrary motion
b. Parallel motion
c. Similar motion
d. Oblique motion

75. What is the name of the highly useful digital interface that allows communication between digital instruments and computers, facilitating ease of composing, arranging, performing, recording, and editing?

a. RAM
b. DAW
c. MIDI
d. MP4

76. How does bow handling on the cello and bass differ from bow handling on the violin and viola?

a. The pinky finger does not rest on top of the bow when playing the cello or bass.
b. The arm generally stays above the bow when playing the cello or bass.
c. The pinky finger rests on top of the bow when playing the cello or bass.
d. The elbow generally stays above the bow when playing the cello or bass.

77. Which trumpet mute, also known by the brand name Harmon mute, produces a buzzed tone and is often associated with Miles Davis during his cool jazz period?

a. Straight mute
b. Wah-wah mute
c. Cup mute
d. Bucket mute

78. What is the name of the playing technique for French horn that produces a slightly darker tone, more easily controls pitch, and aids in performing extended techniques such as stopped horn and echo horn?

a. Left-hand technique
b. Open-fist technique
c. Hand-horn technique
d. Closed-throat technique

79. What is a common accompanying pattern in which chords are played note-by-note successively instead of simultaneously?

a. Arpeggio
b. Scales
c. Blocked chord
d. Ostinato

80. As a general rule, how often should a piano be tuned?

a. Once a year
b. Six times a year
c. Every other year
d. Two to four times a year

81. What is the name of the soft tissue at the top of the mouth cavity that singers raise to produce a relaxed and free sound while also easing register transitions and maintaining the health of the vocal mechanisms?

a. Epiglottis
b. Velum
c. Pharynx
d. Uvula

82. What physiological changes are happening to pubescent students when their voice "cracks"?

a. The pharynx expands and the uvula hardens.
b. The alveolar ridge thickens and the oral cavity widens.
c. The larynx enlarges and the vocal folds lengthen and thicken.
d. The glottis strengthens and hard palate lowers.

83. At what developmental stage does the larynx have the highest placement in the throat?

a. Puberty
b. Adult
c. Adolescence
d. Infancy

84. What is the name of that range within a singer's vocal abilities that resonates in the most aesthetically pleasing manner and is usually the most comfortable to sing?

a. Chest voice
b. Tessitura
c. Falsetto
d. Register

85. What is the general range of the alto voice?

a. F3 to D5
b. C4 to A5
c. B2 to G4
d. E2 to C4

86. If a singer does not control the rate of exhalation, what common problem happens physically when the singer runs out of breath?

a. The diaphragm contracts.
b. The abdominals tighten.
c. The chest collapses.
d. The pharynx dilates.

87. How do sopranos maximize vocal tract resonance at high frequencies to achieve a vibrant sound?

a. By creating less space in the oral cavity and tightening the vocal tract
b. By creating more space in the oral cavity and relaxing the vocal tract
c. By creating less space in the oral cavity and relaxing the vocal tract
d. By creating more space in the oral cavity and tightening the vocal tract

88. A singer rests the tongue forward in the mouth with the tip of the tongue against the bottom teeth in order to create maximum space in the mouth. What is likely the resultant sound?

a. Tinny
b. Dull
c. Bright
d. Resonant

89. What is the mnemonic system that, when combined with hand motions, helps to reinforce the special relationship between pitches for sight-reading?

a. Roman numerals
b. C-clef
c. Solfege
d. Nashville system

90. If a vocal student is told to practice yawning, he or she most likely has the common problem of...

a. Singing with a tight throat.
b. Singing out of tune.
c. Singing with blurred words.
d. Singing without rhythm.

91. Taking in a deep breath over as many counts as possible, holding the breath, and then slowly letting out the air on an "S" sound, over as many counts as possible, is an example of what kind of vocal warm-up?

a. Octave warm-up
b. Falsetto warm-up
c. Tessitura warm-up
d. Breathing warm-up

92. The pyramid model of balance and blend in a vocal ensemble refers to what theory?

a. Louder singers should sing at the same level as softer singers.
b. Higher-pitched singers should sing softer than the lowest pitched singers.
c. Taller singers should stand behind shorter singers.
d. Melodic singers should sing louder than accompanying singers.

93. Vocal resonance is important for an effective vocal solo performance because:

a. It increases breathing capacity.
b. It simulates harmonic overtones.
c. It creates a well-projected sound.
d. It clarifies vocal diction.

94. Of the following choral settings, which is better suited for homophonic pieces but can make it difficult for the singers to hear other parts?

a. Blocked formation
b. Matrix formation
c. Columnar formation
d. Mixed formation

95. What is a benefit of having sectional rehearsals as opposed to having only full rehearsals?

a. The players have to clean, adjust, and tune their instruments together.
b. The players are able to work out their counterpoint on original compositions.
c. The players have the opportunity to work on their sight-reading skills.
d. The players are able to fine-tune their parts together.

96. A conductor is conducting with heavier, slower movements and a grave expression on her face. What sound and mood is the conductor trying to elicit from the ensemble?

a. Dark and somber
b. Quick and energetic
c. Slow and passionate
d. Upbeat and hopeful

97. What is NOT an aspect of the score the conductor needs to learn when preparing a score?

a. Form
b. Transpositions
c. Publisher
d. Dynamics

98. How can conductors best promote cultural diversity in their music programs?

a. Take yearly trips to non-Western countries.
b. Include non-Western musical repertoire into concerts.
c. Have a non-Western music day camp.
d. Assign non-Western textbooks to all the students.

99. How should a conductor's elbow generally be positioned?

a. Raised high above the podium
b. Close to the torso
c. Pointed to the front of the ensemble
d. Slightly raised away from the body

100. What is the main role of the free hand when conducting an ensemble?

a. Keeping the beat
b. Musical reinforcement
c. Balance
d. Following the score

101. Which of the following describes a sequence in which the second segment moves to a different tonal center than the first?

a. Real sequence
b. False sequence
c. Modulating sequence
d. Tonal sequence

102. Which of the following choral structures is the most common for four-part vocal harmony?

a. SATB
b. SAB
c. SSAA
d. TTBB

103. Which of the following improvisational tools is based on a dialogue structure?

a. Repetition
b. Question and answer
c. Syncopation
d. Heterophony

104. When arranging music, which group of instruments would best function as a crisp and bright fanfare?

a. Strings
b. Woodwinds
c. Low brasses
d. High brasses

105. Which of the following notation programs allows musicians to notate compositions electronically and then transfer the data to other MIDI instruments?

a. Mozarteum
b. Sibelius
c. MagicNote
d. Forte Score

106. What component of a stringed instrument generates the sound?

a. The strings
b. The soundboard
c. The bridge
d. The neck

107. When a bow moves faster across a stringed instrument with greater pressure, what sound is produced?

a. A softer dynamic
b. A muted tone
c. A louder dynamic
d. A longer resonance

108. When beginning string players say their pegs do not hold, what is the most common cause?

a. They are not turning the pegs in a clockwise motion.
b. The length of the string is too long for the peg.
c. The instrument has entered an environment that is too humid.
d. They are not putting enough pressure on the end of the peg when turning it.

109. A beginning cello student plays with too much arm movement; what is most likely causing the problem?

a. The student's back is slouched.
b. The elbow is not bending properly on a bow stroke.
c. The thumb is placed too close to the second and third fingers.
d. The fingers are overly curved.

110. Which of the following is NOT a double reed woodwind instrument?

a. Oboe
b. Bassoon
c. Clarinet
d. Sarrusophone

111. What is the most effective technique for woodwind students in developing good intonation?

a. Practicing long tones
b. Practicing in a group
c. Practicing in front of a mirror
d. Practicing rapid scales

112. On reed instruments, reeds that are chipped or cracked should be:

a. Soaked
b. Discarded
c. Sanded
d. Trimmed

113. A beginning student plays the flute with a small and weak tone; what is most likely causing the problem?

a. The student is overblowing.
b. The wrists are bent the wrong way.
c. The lip corners are pulled slightly back.
d. The bottom lip is covering too much of the lip plate.

114. Place the following brass instruments in order from brightest to darkest timbres: French horn, flugelhorn, trumpet, trombone.

a. Flugelhorn, trumpet, French horn, trombone
b. Trumpet, flugelhorn, trombone, French horn
c. Trombone, trumpet, flugelhorn, French horn
d. French horn, flugelhorn, trumpet, trombone

115. Which of the physical aspects of brass performance directly affects changes in dynamics?

a. Embouchure
b. Frequency
c. Posture
d. Volume of air

116. For valved brass instruments that are used nearly daily, how often should valve oil be applied?

a. Only in particularly dry conditions
b. When storing the instrument long-term
c. Two to three times per week
d. After an extended performance

117. Which of the following is the most likely cause for a trumpet student's pitch to fall flat only at the ends of musical phrases?

a. Lack of breath support
b. Mouth corners being too relaxed
c. Neglecting to use the tuning slides
d. The tongue resting too high in the mouth

118. Which percussion instruments are played by striking two objects together?

a. Percussion idiophones
b. Membranophones
c. Concussion idiophones
d. Friction idiophones

119. Which of the following marimba mallet grips provide the most independence for mallet movement?

a. Traditional crossed grip
b. Musser/Stevens grip
c. Two-mallet grip
d. Burton grip

120. How should cymbals be stored?

a. Upright in a sturdy and stiff box
b. Stacked in a dark closet or room
c. Flat in a soundproof and clean locker
d. Divided in padded bags or cases

121. Which of the following is the most likely cause of a buzzing sound when a beginner snare drum student plays fast?

a. The student is hammering the drumstick onto the drum.
b. The student is playing multiple strokes on the drum.
c. The student is dropping the drumstick onto the drum.
d. The student is playing single strokes on the drum.

122. Instrumental warm-ups should:

a. Begin with the most challenging techniques to expedite the process.
b. Begin moderately then gradually increasing the speed, intensity, and range.
c. Begin and maintain slow tempo, low intensity, and a narrow range.
d. Begin with physical stretching and then proceed immediately to repertoire.

123. What is the standard instrumentation of the concert band as prescribed by members of the American Bandmasters Association?

a. Two flutes, two oboes, two bassoons, three clarinets, one bass clarinet, four saxophones, four horns, three trumpets, three trombones, one baritone horn, one tuba, and three or four percussion instruments
b. Four violins, four violas, four cellos, four basses, two piccolos, one English horn, one harp, one bass trombone, one bassoon, one contrabassoon, and two saxophones
c. Four flutes, two piccolos, three oboes, one bassoon, two contrabassoons, four clarinets, three alto clarinets, two bass clarinets, one saxophone, and two percussion instruments
d. Two French horns, two flugelhorns, three trumpets, two cornets, one baritone horn, two tubas, three trombones, three saxophones, and four percussion instruments

124. Which of the following is NOT an important element of an effective solo performance?

a. Dynamics
b. Correct intonation
c. Phrasing
d. Fingerings

125. How often should a conductor check for accurate intonation of the ensemble?

a. Only at the beginning of rehearsals
b. Every third rehearsal
c. Periodically during rehearsals
d. At the end of every rehearsal

126. What plays a direct role in vowel formation and clear diction for singers?

a. The larynx
b. The tongue
c. The lungs
d. The vocal tract

127. How does the hand move when conducting a 4/4 beat pattern?

a. Upward on the first beat, downward on the second beat, inward on the third beat, and outward on the fourth beat
b. Inward on the first beat, outward on the second beat, upward on the third beat, and downward on the fourth beat
c. Outward on the first beat, upward on the second beat, downward on the third beat, and inward on the fourth beat
d. Downward on the first beat, inward on the second beat, outward on the third beat, and upward on the fourth beat

128. Of the following, what is the best technique for using recordings in score study?

a. Listen to a variety of interpretations
b. Use recordings at every rehearsal
c. Listen to famous recordings
d. Practice conducting to the recording

129. What is NOT an aspect to consider when selecting music for an ensemble?

a. Number of rehearsals before the performance
b. Strengths and weaknesses of the ensemble
c. Height of the players in the ensemble
d. Number of players and instruments in the ensemble

130. Which of the following instruments is typically notated on the treble clef and sounds a minor third higher than written?

a. B^b clarinet
b. A clarinet
c. D clarinet
d. E^b clarinet

Answer Key and Explanations

1. D: The note in the example is D-flat. The key signature contains seven flats: Bb, Eb, Ab, Db, Gb, Cb, and Fb; therefore, the answer can be neither choice B nor choice C. The third line of the bass clef is a D, but the key signature indicates that this should be a D-flat; a careless error may result in reading the third line as B, which is only valid in the treble clef.

2. B: *Larghissimo* means "at an extremely broad and slow tempo." Answer A, *andante,* means "at a walking pace." Answer C, *largo,* means "at a very slow tempo," but not as slow as *larghissimo*. Answer D, *larghetto*, is the diminutive of *largo*, and thus not quite as slow as *largo*. The correct answer is B, *larghissimo*.

3. C: When an accent mark is present, it means to play with stress on that note. Staccato means to play with a shortened sound duration. Fermata means to hold a note longer than written, customarily up to twice as long as normal. The correct answer is tenuto, which means to play at full length or slightly longer. Both fermata and tenuto indicate that a musical element should be lengthened; however, a fermata usually indicates a longer pause than tenuto.

4. A: The chord in the given example is an E# diminished triad. In the key of F# major, this chord is built on the seventh scale degree of the F# major scale (F#-G#-A#-B-C#-D#-<u>E#</u>-F#). In standard music theory notation, the E# diminished chord can be written in Roman numerals as vii^{o}, answer A.

5. C: In the treble clef, the lines from bottom to top are: E, G, B, D, F. From the fifth line on the treble clef, the first ledger line above that is an interval of one-third higher. Because the top line is F, an interval of a third up would be A. The correct answer, then, is A#.

6. D: The connected beams suggest groupings of three eighth notes. In compound meter, one beat is composed of three eighth notes (a dotted quarter note), so there are three beats in the measure, making a time signature of 9/8. Of the answer choices, only 9/8 would fit the given example with the correct number of beats. While only two groups of three eighth notes are beamed, the quarter note and eighth note at the beginning add up to one full beat.

7. B: To find the harmony of the chord, the pitches must be stacked in root position so that the note names are a third apart. In the given example, root position would be: A-C-Eb-G. Because the interval between the root and the fifth is a diminished 5th and the distance between the root and the seventh is minor 7th, the harmony of the given chord is A half-diminished 7th.

8. C: To find the interval, count every line and space: line-space-line-space, for an interval of a fourth. The notes in the given example are D and Ab. Because D down to Ab is a half-step greater than a perfect fourth, the correct answer is choice C, augmented fourth. An interval of a perfect fourth would be D down to A or Db down to Ab.

9. A: The chord in the given example has G as its root, so that the chord in root position can be spelled: G-B-D-F#. Because the interval from G to F# is a major seventh, rather than a minor 7th, the chord is a major 7th chord. The 7th note of the chord—F#—is in the bass, which indicates that the chord is in third inversion, thus the correct answer is A: major seventh in third inversion.

10. B: The chords in the example are E major in first inversion, A major in root position, B major in second inversion, and F# minor in root position. In the key of E major, the chords given should be written in Roman numerals relative to their scale degrees in the key (E-F#-G#-A-B-C#-D#): I^6 – IV – $V^6/_4$ – ii.

11. D: The open chords in the given example are Eb major, which is the I chord in the key, and Bb major, which is the V chord. Of the answer choices, the only cadence that ends on a V chord is answer D: half cadence. Perfect authentic cadences progress from V-I; plagal cadences, IV-I; and deceptive cadences, usually from V-VI.

12. A: The mode in the given example is most related to the C major scale, indicated by the major third interval (C to E) and the major sixth and seventh intervals (C to A and C to B, respectively). Of the answer choices, the Lydian mode, answer A is most similar to the major scale, with a raised fourth degree—F# in the example. Dorian, Locrian, and Phrygian modes are most similar to the minor scale.

13. C: The F# dissonance in the given example comes between a G and E, so that the soprano line moves downwards in a step-wise motion. This is an example of a passing tone. A neighbor tone also moves in a stepwise motion but returns to the original tone; a suspension sounds on a downbeat, then moves downward by step; and an appoggiatura is a leap followed by a step.

14. B: The harmonic interval in the example shows G-flat to F-flat. In the major diatonic scale, the 7th interval from G-flat would be F. Because the 7th note is lowered by a half step, it is a minor 7th interval. An augmented 7th would be G-flat to F-sharp, and a diminished 7th would be G-flat to F-double flat.

15. D: In compound meter, the number of pulses can be subdivided into groups of three. Of the answer choices, only answer D can be subdivided into two groups of three. All the other options are examples of simple meters (simple duple, simple triple, simple quadruple).

16. A: The meter in the given example contains seven beats per measure, with the eighth note getting the pulse, indicated by the number "8" on the bottom of the time signature. Because the music is written with two quarter notes in the bass line followed by a dotted quarter, the pulse is best felt with the eighth notes grouped with the bass line: 2-2-3.

17. B: Hemiola is a word that describes rhythms that are contrasted in a 3:2 ratio, most commonly exemplified by having 3 beats occupy the space that is ordinarily given 2 beats. In the given example, the treble notes shift from groupings of 3 to groupings of 2 in 6/8 meter, which gives a sense of meter change from triple to duple. This is an example of the less common form of hemiola known as horizontal hemiola. Anacrusis refers to notes before the downbeat of the first measure, suspension refers to voice leading within tonal harmony, and augmentation refers to rhythmic lengthening.

18. A: Of the answer choices, staccatissimo has the shortest duration. Staccato indicates that the note should be played short but not as short as staccatissimo. Tenuto indicates that the note should be played for its full length or slightly longer. Accent indicates that the note should be played with a strong stress.

19. D: The waltz is a dance form that features triple meter in a lively tempo. Musical aspects of the waltz help dancers feel the motion of the turn. In waltz time, the rhythmic emphasis is on the downbeat, while the other two beats are kept light, similarly to the steps within the dance. The correct answer is D, the first beat.

20. C: The answer choices all have to do with a change in tempo; however, only one indicates a quickening of the tempo. *Affrettando*, the correct answer, comes from Italian, meaning "to hurry." *Slentando* also comes from Italian, meaning "to slow down;" *allargando* comes from Italian, meaning "to widen;" and *calando* comes from Italian, meaning "to let down."

21. B: In the given example, the bass repeats a rhythmic pattern on the same note, similarly to a drone. This is an example of a rhythmic ostinato, a short, constantly repeating rhythmic pattern. A 3-2 clave would have a rhythm of three followed by a rhythm of two, a bossa nova is also a specific rhythmic pattern that would be repeated in different harmonies, and an Alberti bass refers to a bass figuration that outlines the tones within a triad.

22. C: Rondo form is defined by a principal theme (A) in the tonic key that alternates with episodes (B and C). The five-part rondo is usually described as ABACA. The 7-part rondo is usually described as ABACABA, which is answer C. Answer A describes chain form. Answer B is not a generally recognized musical form. Answer D is ternary form.

23. B: Compound musical form describes a tonal work that can be seen as a composite of other, smaller, simple forms such as binary and ternary forms. Sonata form, minuetto and trio, and rondo form are all composed of multiple distinct sections or movements. The only answer choice that is not a compound form is binary form, answer choice B.

24. B: The original literary form of the *ballade* usually featured a narrative that was comic, romantic, tragic, or historical; words were set to three stanzas with seven or eight lines each. Musical *ballades* were not based on literary forms of plays, soliloquies, or elegies.

25. C: The *opera seria* that arose during the Enlightenment focused on tragic and serious subjects. The structure, number of singers, and plot line were structured so that the action usually took place in three acts with alternating arias and recitatives, and the number of characters usually numbered six or seven with two to four main characters.

26. A: Dialogue, also known as call and response, is an important stylistic element of the African musical tradition. The call and response form has been widely influential in music such as blues, jazz, hip hop, rock, and gospel. Modes can be traced to the ancient Greek tradition, discant is an element of Medieval music, and coda refers to musical form within Western classical music.

27. B: A tone cluster is defined as a group of closely spaced notes played simultaneously, usually in intervals of adjacent seconds and groupings, or "clusters." Extended harmony and a diminished seventh have notes that are spaced more widely than adjacent seconds, and retrograde inversion refers to twelve-tone music technique.

28. A: Of the given answer choices, the best answer is Baroque music. Baroque music was traditionally improvised, as in jazz music, and followed a standard in performance, whether a 32-bar form in jazz or a ritornello form in Baroque music. In both genres, improvisations are based on outlined chord symbols that direct the melody.

29. D: Organum is an early form of polyphony developed during the Medieval period in which voices were sung in parallel motion. The motet evolved from organum and featured a tenor line with contrasting upper voices. Gregorian chant has melodies with no meter, and masses are large-scale works that also feature polyphony in counterpoint.

30. B: Nationalism, as the name implies, was the name of the movement in the Romantic era in which composers used folk melodies of their country within their compositions. Impressionism focused on capturing the moods and emotions of a subject though texture, musical "color," ambiguous harmony, among other techniques. Romanticism focused on music that portrayed fantastical, emotional, and dramatic subjects. Realism was primarily an artistic and literary movement that focused on portraying subjects in a non-idealized, realistic style.

31. C: Arnold Schoenberg developed the twelve-tone technique of music in which all twelve pitches of the chromatic scale are treated as equal. Anton Webern, Milton Babbit, and Pierre Boulez were composers who subsequently used the twelve-tone technique in their compositions, but they did not create it.

32. A: Absolute music is defined as instrumental music that exists apart from extra-musical references. Programmatic music is music that can be represented by non-musical images or ideas. Of the answer choices, only answer A, *Symphony No. 5* by Ludwig van Beethoven, exists apart from extra-musical references.

33. B: Music of the Baroque era featured heavy ornamentation and improvised embellishment of a musical line. Music of the Classical era featured restraint, lighter texture, objectivity, and a transparent melodic line. Music of the Romantic era featured expressive emotionalism, and music of the 20th and 21st centuries featured modernism and rejection of tonality.

34. A: In the Baroque era, strings and winds were often doubled to play certain lines. With the new Classical era, first violins were the dominant string section, while the lower strings became the supporting background harmonically and rhythmically. The bassoon became increasingly independent as opposed to the previous Baroque setting of the bassoon as part of the bass line.

35. D: Igor Stravinsky wrote music that featured brass with large orchestrations and increasingly powerful orchestral sounds in monumental compositions such as *The Firebird, Petrushka,* and *The Rite of Spring.* While the other composers also wrote for orchestra, including brass, they are not as closely associated with powerful orchestral sounds as Stravinksy.

36. C: Typical instruments used in Appalachian music include the banjo, mandolin, guitar, autoharp, American fiddle, fretted dulcimer, dobros, and dulcimer. The tumbadora, another name for the conga, is a drum from Cuba used in mambo, rumba, and many other Latin musical styles.

37. B: Historians mark *Show Boat* (1927) by Kern and Hammerstein as the first Broadway musical with a fully integrated, serious, continuous plot. Before *Show Boat,* Broadway plays consisted of musical comedies and operettas without serious narratives. *Cats* by Andrew Lloyd Webber premiered in 1981; *Ain't Misbehavin'* by Horwitz and Maltby, Jr. premiered in 1978; and *Porgy and Bess* by George Gershwin opened in 1935.

38. D: New Orleans jazz, developed at the start of the 20th century, was one of the earliest forms of jazz music, borrowing from the music of black and creole musicians. West Coast jazz was developed in the 1950s, Kansas City blues was developed in the 1920s and 1930s, and Latin jazz was developed in the 1940s and 1950s.

39. A: In their 1979 hit single *Rapper's Delight,* The Sugarhill Gang helped to popularize the term "hip hop" into mainstream culture. The lyrics read: "I said a hip hop, hippie to the hippie, the hip, hip a hop, and you don't stop, a rock it to the bang bang boogie, say, up jump the boogie, to the rhythm of the boogie, the beat."

40. D: Blues music was heavily influenced by the black church through improvisation, storytelling, call and response, vocal inflections, and the blues progression. Many of these musical features are now representative of the blues genre of music.

41. A: Cajun music of Louisiana traces its roots back to French musical traditions. Early French settlers on the North American continent migrated from New Brunswick and Nova Scotia to southern Louisiana and brought with them traditional French ballads that, over time, developed into present-day Cajun music.

42. C: Although funk, soul, and R&B are all inspired by the African musical tradition, funk differs from soul and R&B because it is based mainly on a rhythmic groove and bass lines over simple chords, rather than on a melody line or a progression over many chords, as in soul and R&B.

43. B: The cha-cha-cha is an onomatopoeia of the musical rhythm: two eighth notes followed by a quarter note. The tresillo is comprised of triplets over a composite duple beat. The son montuno is comprised of a 2-3 clave, and the rumba rhythmic pattern consists of 16th and quarter note beats in triple- and duple-pulses.

44. A: Call and response singing, polyrhythms, and improvised rhythms are all common features of music from Africa, answer A. Music from Asian cultures can feature polyrhythms and improvised rhythms, but is not known for call and response singing. Traditional music from Europe and North America do not feature call and response singing, polyrhythms, or improvised rhythms.

45. D: *Kabuki* is the name of the Japanese theater form that stems from the Edo period of the 1600s. *Kesho* is the name of the white and dramatic kabuki makeup. *Shosagoto* are kabuki dance pieces, one of three types of kabuki. *Michiyuki* is a section of the kabuki play that includes a journey scene where characters dance or talk while travelling.

46. C: The *maqam* system of melodic organization used in Middle Eastern music most resembles the Western mode. There are more than 30 different *maqamat*, and each defines the melodic contour, pitches, and hierarchical development of the scale.

47. D: An ostinato is defined as a short, repeating accompaniment pattern throughout a musical work that can consist of a simple rhythmic, melodic, or harmonic idea. Similar to a drone, the ostinato provides a stable foundation for the main melody line. Ostinatos are found extensively in sub-Saharan African world music, including Ethiopian music.

48. D: Reggae music originated in the Caribbean nation of Jamaica in the 1960s. The music has roots in traditional calypso and mento music as well as in American jazz, rhythm and blues, ska, and the rocksteady movement of the 60s. Early Jamaican reggae musicians include Jackie Mittoo, Winston Wright, "Scratch" Perry, and The Pioneers.

49. C: Apartheid was the name of the system of racial segregation and discrimination enforced by white rule in South Africa for 46 years. During that time, freedom songs were used to unite the oppressed and expose the injustices of the government during that period of hatred and brutality.

50. A: The term *leitmotif* is used to identify a reoccurring motivic fragment that musically represents some part of a musical drama, usually a person, place, or idea. The leitmotif is a useful tool for composers: character development, the unfolding of the story, reinforcement of the action taking place onstage, and recalling an event or person from a previous scene are all techniques of the leitmotif.

51. C: Composers typically use the minor mode to convey sadness in a piece of music. The major mode is most often associated with happiness or cheerfulness, with its interval of a major third. The Mixolydian and Lydian modes sound similar to the major mode, except that the Mixolydian mode has a lowered seventh scale degree, and the Lydian mode has a raised fourth scale degree.

52. D: A loud, forceful, and fast sound tends to convey passion, answer D. Sorrow tends to be represented by slower sounds; calm is usually represented by slower, light sounds; and hope tends to be represented by sustained, high sounds.

53. B: The system of music education through movement called eurythmics was developed around 1900 by Swiss composer, musician, and pedagogue Émile Jaques-Dalcroze, in which students use a kinesthetic approach to experience musical concepts. The body is seen as the instrument, and students discover musicality, tempo, dynamics, and phrase structure through physical dialogue with the music.

54. C: When encountering a difficult passage, musicians most effectively practice that passage slowly and thoughtfully. Playing through a challenging passage quickly can be detrimental to the learning process. Studying away from the instrument and practicing the sections before and after can be helpful, but will not address the difficult passage in the most effective manner.

55. B: An orchestrator would most likely choose strings to represent a lush canvas of passionate sound. String instruments can sustain sound unlike percussion instruments, and with an entire section of strings, the timbre of the instruments coupled with the ease of tremolo and slide technique would easily represent a lush and passionate sound.

56. A: The staccato articulation would best evoke a sense of raindrops, with its short and light sound texture. A legato articulation is smooth and connected, unlike the short drops of rain. A tenuto articulation is held longer than a staccato and would also not represent raindrops as well. A fermata articulation means to hold a note for an extended period of time.

57. D: Musical phrasing, contour, and line can be most analogous to the cadence and inflection of language in a narrated text. Many musical analogies relate to the spoken word, such as "call and response" or "question and answer." Musical phrasing, contour, and line are all found in the cadence of language.

58. A: The Fibonacci sequence is a mathematical series where each number in the series is the sum of the two numbers preceding it. These numbers are in a proportion that arises spontaneously in many natural and man-made works. Of the answer choices, the sequence can be found in all musical examples except for answer A: the syncopation of dance forms with the golden ratio.

59. B: A performer's decision to add dramatic intent within a certain musical piece is conceptually most similar to an actor's personal interpretation of character lines. Just as a performer chooses how to interpret the dynamics and markings of a musical work, an actor similarly chooses how to deliver the lines of his or her character.

60. C: The structure of sonata form features three main sections: exposition, development, and recapitulation. This is similar to the setup, conflict, and resolution of literary narrative structure. In both the setup and exposition, the main idea is introduced. In the development and conflict, the melody and plot lines progress. In the recapitulation and resolution, both melody and plot lines resolve at the end.

61. C: The overtone series can be best understood within the context of physics, the study of matter and its motion through space and time. The concept of overtones refers to a specific acoustic property of sound. For every one frequency, there are multiple other frequencies, or overtones, that vibrate through the resonant space of its normal modes.

62. A: The Impressionist music movement of the 19th and 20th centuries paralleled the visual arts movement of Édouard Manet, Claude Monet, Edgar Degas, Pierre-Auguste Renoir, Berthe Morisot, Camille Pissarro, Alfred Sisley, and Mary Cassatt. Both painters and composers abandoned formal elements and created works that caught the soft, brief, and sensory effects of a particular moment.

63. D: The rhythms of music are most related to the steps taken in dance. The size of canvas in a painting would relate more to the length or orchestration of a piece, the shape of a sculpture would relate more to the structure of a musical piece, and the climax of the plot in a novel would relate more to the climax of music.

64. B: A career in music business would include the job title of (B), publicist. Other related job titles are publisher, media promotion specialist, event promoter, arts writer, product manager, recording studio manager, artist scout, account executive, finance assistant, artist liaison, tour manager, booking agent, radio promoter, and music licensing supervisor.

65. D: Performing arts medicine is concerned with overseeing and promoting the health of the performing artist. Medical health professionals evaluate and treat any medical problems that may occur in the performing artist. The focus is to prevent re-injury, and treatment may also cover technique, repertoire, instrument state, and emotional state adjustments, as related to the injury.

66. A: Recording technology coursework would be most important to an aspiring audio engineer. Music theory would be most important to an aspiring composer, physics would be most important to an aspiring acoustician, and music business would be most important to an aspiring music publisher.

67. C: The minimum education requirement for those wishing to enter a career in music education is a bachelor's degree in music education, with the proper state teaching certification. Music educators, whose goal is to teach in conservatory or university, should aim for a doctorate or terminal degree in music to be considered for most tenured professorships.

68. B: The main incentives for aspiring performers to compete in local, regional, and national competitions are performance opportunities and publicity. As an aspiring performer, the additional performances and publicity gained from placing in competitions will help with college admissions, which in turn will help with long-term career and financial goals.

69. C: Military musicians have the most secure job in music, with extensive opportunities to tour, record, and perform at high-profile ceremonies as well as college repayment, health care, and other benefits. The Army, Navy, Air Force, and Coast Guard all have full-time music ensembles. Ensembles are characterized as either premier bands or regional bands.

70. D: Diversifying his or her skill set would best help a music producer with career advancement in an increasingly competitive environment. Although increasing social media marketing, having the latest audio technology, and having a master's degree in music may help somewhat, being able to perform as many skills as possible would best help a music producer with career advancement.

71. A: Of the answer choices, the fugue is a monothematic composition in which a single subject is continually echoed throughout the piece through imitation and development. The fugue theme is introduced at the beginning of the work, also known as the exposition, and is echoed in all of the fugal voices in different pitches and various keys.

72. D: When harmonizing any given melody, analysis should first be done before any planning, sketching, or execution of harmonization. The musician should first observe the contour of the melody and analyze what possible harmonies can be written with regard to the pitches and rhythmic structure.

73. B: Imitation is a foundational tool for beginning improvisation. Imitation allows students to learn techniques, progressions, melodic contour, and rhythmic patterns of improvisers of the past. Once students have immersed themselves in studying imitation, they will be much better suited to assimilate improvisation techniques for new musical ideas.

74. D: Oblique motion refers to the motion of two musical lines in which one line stays stationary while the other musical line moves in an upward or downward direction. Contrary motion moves in opposite directions, parallel motion moves in the same direction, and similar motion refers to the motion of two musical lines that move in similar directions.

75. C: MIDI is the name of the highly useful digital interface that allows communication between digital instruments and computers, facilitating ease of composing, arranging, performing, recording, and editing. Short for Musical Instrument Digital Interface, it does not record a digital version of a sound recording but instead stores performance data of a particular performance, such as key presses, velocity, and pedal movements.

76. A: On the cello and bass, the pinky finger does not rest on top of the bow as on the violin and viola bow; instead, the pinky should rest next to the middle and ring fingers. Because both the cello and bass are played upright, the arm does not generally stay above the bow; in fact, bow handling on a cello and bass requires the elbow and arm to lower significantly.

77. B: The wah-wah mute, also known by the brand name Harmon mute, produces a buzzed tone and is often associated with Miles Davis during his cool jazz period. The straight mute results in a tinny, metallic sound; the cup mute produces a muffled, darker tone; and the bucket mute produces a softer tone and reduces the piercing quality of loud or high notes that can be amplified by other mutes.

78. C: Hand-horn technique, also known as right hand technique, is the placement of the right hand inside the bell of the horn to produce a slightly darker tone, to more easily control pitch, and to perform extended techniques such as stopped horn and echo horn.

79. A: An arpeggio is defined as a chord that is played note-by-note, successively, instead of simultaneously. Also termed as a broken chord, the arpeggio can be played from the highest note to the lowest note, but is more commonly played from the lowest note to the highest note.

80. D: As a general rule, pianos should be tuned between two to four times a year. This depends on the seasonal temperature and humidity changes as well as the frequency of piano use, but two to four times a year generally ensures that the piano stays maintained and in tune.

81. B: The soft tissue at the top of the mouth cavity that singers raise to produce a relaxed and free sound while also easing register transitions and maintaining the health of the vocal mechanisms is called the velum. When singers lift the soft palate, the resulting space within the oral cavity enlarges, helping to achieve a more resonant, warm tone without restrictions

82. C: Voice development will affect vocal students as the larynx enlarges and the vocal folds lengthen and thicken. The physiological changes of the vocal mechanisms tend to affect boys more than girls, evident in the "cracking" of the voice. During puberty, students will have to work towards singing voice production, pitch accuracy, and increasing vocal range.

83. D: Until puberty, a child's vocal mechanisms are not fully developed and do not contain the full range of the adult voice. Infants are born with a very high larynx; the larynx drops slightly when a child reaches the age of three. During puberty, a child's larynx grows to its full size, drops, and the vocal cords lengthen and thicken substantially.

84. B: Tessitura refers to that range within a singer's vocal abilities that resonates in the most aesthetically pleasing manner and that is generally the most comfortable for the singer. Tessitura differs from vocal range in that the range of a singer's voice refers to the limits of pitches the singer is able to sing.

85. A: The general vocal range of the alto voice is from F3 to D5. The general vocal range of the soprano voice is from C4, middle C, to A5; the general vocal range of the tenor voice is from B2 to G4; and the general vocal range of the bass voice is from E2 to C4. Although many composers use these ranges in writing a piece of four-part harmony, each individual's voice can vary drastically in range and ability.

86. C: If a singer does not control the rate of exhalation, a collapsed chest is a common problem that happens. After the inhalation, the singer must control the rate of exhalation, as the flow of air through the vocal cords results in sound. The singer must use great care to manage the rate of airflow by engaging the abdominal muscles to achieve a steady stream of air through the trachea and larynx.

87. B: Many sopranos will maximize vocal tract resonance at high frequencies by creating more space in the oral cavity and relaxing the vocal tract so that the resultant sound is vibrant and sonorous. The vocal tract has optimal resonances for certain frequencies, and it is important for the singer to maximize the resonances of the vibrating vocal tract with the specific pitch frequencies.

88. D: This tongue position is generally used to create a resonant sound. The tongue should always be kept relaxed and free from tension when singing to avoid a choked sound and possible injury to the vocal mechanisms.

89. C: Solfege uses syllables that are assigned to the notes of a musical scale to aid musicians in mentally hearing the pitches of written music. Solfege should be reinforced by singing through a number of different keys to train the ears to hear the relationships between the diatonic pitches.

90. A: If a vocal student is told to practice yawning, he or she most likely has the common problem of singing with a tight throat. The yawn helps the throat to achieve its most open and relaxed state, necessary for productive and healthy singing.

91. D: This is an example of a breathing warm-up. Breathing warm-ups engage the diaphragm for supported singing and help to warm the vocal cords for singing.

92. B: The pyramid model of balance and blend refers to the theory that higher pitched singers and instruments should play softer than the lowest pitched singers and instruments so that an ideal balance exists between the treble and the bass. In this model, the higher pitched section will also be able to hear the bass for better intonation and blend.

93. C: Vocal resonance is important for an effective vocal solo performance because it creates a well-projected sound. Singing in the proper vocal register without strain, with strong vocal cords, and with the tongue and mouth in position to maximize resonance helps to project the singing voice.

94. A: The choral sound from a blocked formation tends to be better suited for homophonic pieces but can make it difficult for the singers to hear other parts. In the blocked formation, the vocal parts are solidly separated from front to back so that all sopranos are grouped at one end from front row to back row, altos are grouped next, then the tenors, and lastly the basses.

95. D: Sectional rehearsals allow players to fine-tune their parts together and to fix any technical or musical problems apart from the full ensemble. Sometimes, the conductor may not be aware of other hidden problems except through listening to sectional rehearsals.

96. A: A skilled conductor is able to extract the appropriate musical expression from the ensemble with the slightest of gestures. The conductor should utilize his or her entire body in conveying the musical expression of the piece. Slow movements and a grave expression indicate a dark and somber mood.

97. C: The publisher is not an aspect of the score the conductor needs to learn when preparing a score; however, the form, transpositions, and dynamics of the score are all necessary aspects of the score to learn when preparing a score for rehearsals and performances.

98. B: Conductors can promote cultural diversity in their music programs by including non-Western musical repertoire into their concerts. Although yearly international trips may sound appealing, it is neither practical nor cost-effective. Neither devoting only a day to non-Western music nor assigning textbooks to students effectively promotes cultural diversity within a music program.

99. D: A conductor's elbow should be positioned so that it is slightly raised away from the body. The baton can then be best and clearly seen from all angles. It should not be raised high above the podium, close to the torso, nor pointed to the front of the ensemble; the baton should be a natural extension of the hand and arm.

100. B: The main role of the free hand when conducting an ensemble is as musical reinforcement. As an independent stimulus, the free hand can reinforce dynamics such as crescendos and decrescendos as well as aid in cueing parts. The free hand should also indicate releases, phrasing, musical style, and necessary modifications in the balance of the ensemble.

101. C: A modulating sequence is a sequence in which the second segment moves to a different tonal center than the first. A real sequence is one in which the second segment is an exact intervallic transposition of the first. A false sequence is one in which only a part of the first segment is transposed. A tonal sequence is one in which the first segment is transposed but kept within the diatonic scale.

102. A: The most common choral structure for four-part vocal harmony is SATB (soprano, alto, tenor, bass). SAB only makes use of three voices, and SSAA and TTBB are not as commonly used as SATB.

103. B: The question and answer improvisational tool is based on dialogue structure. As in dialogue within language, there is interplay between speakers and lines: a musical line "responds" to a previous musical line, and this response can come from a different musician, instrument, group, or register within a solo performer.

104. D: When arranging music, high brasses would best function as a crisp and bright fanfare. Fanfares are closely associated with brass instruments. Woodwinds lack the penetrating power of high brass, so they are not the best choice. Strings also are not as closely associated with fanfare and are not as bright as high brasses. Low brasses would not provide as bright a tone as high brasses.

105. B: Sibelius is notation software that allows musicians to notate compositions electronically and then transfer the data to other MIDI instruments. Other similar programs include MuseScore, Dorico, and Finale. Using notation software helps to reinforce musical concepts and compositional lessons for students.

106. A: The strings of a stringed instrument generate the sound. As the strings are set in motion, they vibrate the surrounding air as well as the soundboard through the bridge as a resonant vibrator, and an audible tone effuses out of the instrument through the sound hole.

107. C: When a bow moves faster across a stringed instrument with greater pressure, a louder dynamic is produced. When playing louder dynamics such as *forte, fortissimo,* and *mezzo forte*, the bow must move faster across the strings with greater pressure to produce greater amplitudes in the vibrating sound waves.

108. D: When beginning string players say their pegs do not hold, the most common cause is that they are not putting enough pressure on the end of the peg when turning it. Correctly winding the strings on the pegs is very important for the pegs to work correctly. Students should imagine the peg as having screw threads with which to wind the peg.

109. B: A beginning cello student who plays with too much arm movement is most likely not bending the elbow properly on a bow stroke. When bowing on a cello, students should use not only their upper arms, but also their forearms, elbows, wrists, hands, and fingers as well. A stiff elbow causes too much arm movement during a bow stroke.

110. C: Double reed woodwind instruments produce sound when air is blown through two reeds that are tied together and vibrate. Double reed instruments include the oboe, bassoon, and sarrusophone. The clarinet is a single reed instrument, not a double reed instrument.

111. A: Although all answer choices are helpful practice techniques, woodwind students should practice long tones to develop good intonation. The benefit of the exercise lies in removing other aspects of performance such as reading, fingering, and so on, allowing the player to singly direct his or her focus towards the production of those aspects that create a pleasing tone.

112. B: On reed instruments, reeds that are chipped or cracked should be discarded. There is usually not a way to repair chipped or cracked reeds. Players should always keep spare reeds nearby for backup and practice proper reed maintenance to prolong the life of each reed.

113. D: A beginning student who plays the flute with a small and weak tone is most likely letting his or her bottom lip cover too much of the lip plate. This prevents a strong and steady stream of air to flow through the mouthpiece, and the resulting sound is small and weak.

114. B: These are the brass instruments given in order from brightest to darkest timbres: trumpet, flugelhorn, trombone, and French horn. The size and aspect of the conical bore affects the instrument's timbre, and of the four instruments, trumpets have the narrowest and most cylindrical bore, while the French horn has the widest and biggest bore.

115. D: Brass instruments typically produce sound through the buzzing of the player's lips as the air travels through the instrument. The lips act as a vibrating valve that produces oscillating air and pressure. Changes in dynamics for the brass instruments are a product of the volume of air moving through the instrument. Embouchure primarily impacts tone and pitch. Frequency refers to the frequency of a sound wave, which determines pitch. Posture can impact pitch, tone, or volume, but the volume of air has a more direct impact on dynamics than posture.

116. C: For valved brass instruments, a small amount of valve oil should be applied a few times a week or before each playing session to prevent parts from seizing. Clean and lubricate all slides, removing old lubricant before applying a new layer, and use only a small amount, removing any excess with a soft cloth. Brass instruments should not be over-oiled, but they do generally need frequent oiling with use. Depending on the player and the instrument, an instrument may even need to be oiled daily or even in the middle of a longer performance.

117. A: The most likely cause for a trumpet student's pitch to fall flat only at the ends of musical phrases is a lack of proper breath support. Without a steady stream of air supported by the diaphragm and proper embouchure, the tendency is for pitches to fall flat only at the ends of musical phrases when the student runs out of breath.

118. C: Concussion idiophones are percussion instruments that are played by striking two objects together. Percussion idiophones are those struck by mallets, membranophones are percussion instruments that produce sound through the vibration of a membrane around a resonating body, and friction idiophones are played by rubbing and include the musical saw and the glass harmonica.

119. B: The Musser/Stevens marimba mallet grip provides the most independence for mallet movement. It places the first mallet between the thumb and index fingers, and the second mallet between the middle and ring fingers so that the mallets are not crossed.

120. D: Cymbals should be stored divided in padded bags or cases, if possible. They should never be stacked directly on top of each other, or upright on their edges, for the risk of damage. The padding helps to protect the cymbal metal and to prolong the life of each cymbal.

121. A: If a beginner snare drum student produces a buzzing sound when playing fast, he or she is most likely hammering the drumstick onto the drum instead of allowing the drumstick to drop or bounce without tension. The snare player should grip the drumstick firmly yet in a relaxed manner so that each stroke has a flowing yet controlled movement with a full, legato sound.

122. B: Instrumental warm-ups should begin moderately then gradually increase the speed, intensity, and range. The warm-up promotes blood flow to the entire body, lubricating all music-making muscles and joints. Starting moderately and increasing the speed, intensity, and range helps to prepare both the player and the instrument.

123. A: The American Bandmasters Association prescribed the concert band as having parts for two flutes, two oboes, two bassoons, three clarinets, one bass clarinet, four saxophones, four horns, three trumpets, three trombones, one baritone horn, one tuba, and three or four percussion instruments. The brass, woodwind family, and percussion instrument families are all represented.

124. D: Of the given answer choices, fingerings are not an important element of an effective solo performance. Fingerings are a useful tool for playing passages efficiently and with ease. However, without dynamics, correct intonation, and tasteful phrasing, the essence of the music will not be effectively conveyed to an audience.

125. C: During a rehearsal, the director should periodically check for accurate intonation of the ensemble. Aside from beginning each rehearsal with accurate tuning, the director should isolate each different section for intonation spot checks. This teaches the students to listen attentively to themselves and also to the surrounding students.

126. B: The tongue plays a key role in vowel formation and clear diction, as it directly influences the vocal tract and the larynx. With all other vocal mechanisms fixed, a change in the tongue directly changes the vocal sound from dull and distorted to tinny and harsh. Clarity in singing requires clear vowel formation so that the words are intelligible to the listening audience.

127. D: When conducting, the downbeat of the pattern always indicates the strongest pulse of the pattern and is indicated by a downward stroke of the hand. The last beat of the pattern is always the weakest pulse of the pattern and is thus indicated by an upward stroke of the hand. In a 4/4 pattern then, the hand moves downward on the first beat, inward on the second beat, outward on the third beat, and upward on the fourth beat.

128. A: When using recordings in score study, careful discretion must be made so that the conductor does not merely copy the interpretation of the recording. The conductor should listen to a variety of interpretations. The conductor should not practice conducting to the recording, should not listen only to famous recordings, and should stop listening to recordings once rehearsals have begun to be able to develop one's own interpretation.

129. C: When a conductor selects music for an ensemble, he or she should consider the number of rehearsals before the performance, the strengths and weaknesses of the ensemble, and the number of players and instruments in the ensemble. The conductor should NOT consider the height of the players in the ensemble, answer choice C.

130. D: The E^{b} clarinet is typically notated on the treble clef and sounds a minor third higher than written. The B^{b} clarinet sounds a major second lower than written; the A clarinet sounds a minor third lower than written; and the D clarinet sounds a major second higher than written, all with a range of E3-C7.

How to Overcome Test Anxiety

Just the thought of taking a test is enough to make most people a little nervous. A test is an important event that can have a long-term impact on your future, so it's important to take it seriously and it's natural to feel anxious about performing well. But just because anxiety is normal, that doesn't mean that it's helpful in test taking, or that you should simply accept it as part of your life. Anxiety can have a variety of effects. These effects can be mild, like making you feel slightly nervous, or severe, like blocking your ability to focus or remember even a simple detail.

If you experience test anxiety—whether severe or mild—it's important to know how to beat it. To discover this, first you need to understand what causes test anxiety.

Causes of Test Anxiety

While we often think of anxiety as an uncontrollable emotional state, it can actually be caused by simple, practical things. One of the most common causes of test anxiety is that a person does not feel adequately prepared for their test. This feeling can be the result of many different issues such as poor study habits or lack of organization, but the most common culprit is time management. Starting to study too late, failing to organize your study time to cover all of the material, or being distracted while you study will mean that you're not well prepared for the test. This may lead to cramming the night before, which will cause you to be physically and mentally exhausted for the test. Poor time management also contributes to feelings of stress, fear, and hopelessness as you realize you are not well prepared but don't know what to do about it.

Other times, test anxiety is not related to your preparation for the test but comes from unresolved fear. This may be a past failure on a test, or poor performance on tests in general. It may come from comparing yourself to others who seem to be performing better or from the stress of living up to expectations. Anxiety may be driven by fears of the future—how failure on this test would affect your educational and career goals. These fears are often completely irrational, but they can still negatively impact your test performance.

Elements of Test Anxiety

As mentioned earlier, test anxiety is considered to be an emotional state, but it has physical and mental components as well. Sometimes you may not even realize that you are suffering from test anxiety until you notice the physical symptoms. These can include trembling hands, rapid heartbeat, sweating, nausea, and tense muscles. Extreme anxiety may lead to fainting or vomiting. Obviously, any of these symptoms can have a negative impact on testing. It is important to recognize them as soon as they begin to occur so that you can address the problem before it damages your performance.

The mental components of test anxiety include trouble focusing and inability to remember learned information. During a test, your mind is on high alert, which can help you recall information and stay focused for an extended period of time. However, anxiety interferes with your mind's natural processes, causing you to blank out, even on the questions you know well. The strain of testing during anxiety makes it difficult to stay focused, especially on a test that may take several hours. Extreme anxiety can take a huge mental toll, making it difficult not only to recall test information but even to understand the test questions or pull your thoughts together.

Effects of Test Anxiety

Test anxiety is like a disease—if left untreated, it will get progressively worse. Anxiety leads to poor performance, and this reinforces the feelings of fear and failure, which in turn lead to poor performances on subsequent tests. It can grow from a mild nervousness to a crippling condition. If allowed to progress, test anxiety can have a big impact on your schooling, and consequently on your future.

Test anxiety can spread to other parts of your life. Anxiety on tests can become anxiety in any stressful situation, and blanking on a test can turn into panicking in a job situation. But fortunately, you don't have to let anxiety rule your testing and determine your grades. There are a number of relatively simple steps you can take to move past anxiety and function normally on a test and in the rest of life.

Physical Steps for Beating Test Anxiety

While test anxiety is a serious problem, the good news is that it can be overcome. It doesn't have to control your ability to think and remember information. While it may take time, you can begin taking steps today to beat anxiety.

Just as your first hint that you may be struggling with anxiety comes from the physical symptoms, the first step to treating it is also physical. Rest is crucial for having a clear, strong mind. If you are tired, it is much easier to give in to anxiety. But if you establish good sleep habits, your body and mind will be ready to perform optimally, without the strain of exhaustion. Additionally, sleeping well helps you to retain information better, so you're more likely to recall the answers when you see the test questions.

Getting good sleep means more than going to bed on time. It's important to allow your brain time to relax. Take study breaks from time to time so it doesn't get overworked, and don't study right before bed. Take time to rest your mind before trying to rest your body, or you may find it difficult to fall asleep.

Along with sleep, other aspects of physical health are important in preparing for a test. Good nutrition is vital for good brain function. Sugary foods and drinks may give a burst of energy but this burst is followed by a crash, both physically and emotionally. Instead, fuel your body with protein and vitamin-rich foods.

Also, drink plenty of water. Dehydration can lead to headaches and exhaustion, especially if your brain is already under stress from the rigors of the test. Particularly if your test is a long one, drink water during the breaks. And if possible, take an energy-boosting snack to eat between sections.

Along with sleep and diet, a third important part of physical health is exercise. Maintaining a steady workout schedule is helpful, but even taking 5-minute study breaks to walk can help get your blood pumping faster and clear your head. Exercise also releases endorphins, which contribute to a positive feeling and can help combat test anxiety.

When you nurture your physical health, you are also contributing to your mental health. If your body is healthy, your mind is much more likely to be healthy as well. So take time to rest, nourish your body with healthy food and water, and get moving as much as possible. Taking these physical steps will make you stronger and more able to take the mental steps necessary to overcome test anxiety.

Mental Steps for Beating Test Anxiety

Working on the mental side of test anxiety can be more challenging, but as with the physical side, there are clear steps you can take to overcome it. As mentioned earlier, test anxiety often stems from lack of preparation, so the obvious solution is to prepare for the test. Effective studying may be the most important weapon you have for beating test anxiety, but you can and should employ several other mental tools to combat fear.

First, boost your confidence by reminding yourself of past success—tests or projects that you aced. If you're putting as much effort into preparing for this test as you did for those, there's no reason you should expect to fail here. Work hard to prepare; then trust your preparation.

Second, surround yourself with encouraging people. It can be helpful to find a study group, but be sure that the people you're around will encourage a positive attitude. If you spend time with others who are anxious or cynical, this will only contribute to your own anxiety. Look for others who are motivated to study hard from a desire to succeed, not from a fear of failure.

Third, reward yourself. A test is physically and mentally tiring, even without anxiety, and it can be helpful to have something to look forward to. Plan an activity following the test, regardless of the outcome, such as going to a movie or getting ice cream.

When you are taking the test, if you find yourself beginning to feel anxious, remind yourself that you know the material. Visualize successfully completing the test. Then take a few deep, relaxing breaths and return to it. Work through the questions carefully but with confidence, knowing that you are capable of succeeding.

Developing a healthy mental approach to test taking will also aid in other areas of life. Test anxiety affects more than just the actual test—it can be damaging to your mental health and even contribute to depression. It's important to beat test anxiety before it becomes a problem for more than testing.

Study Strategy

Being prepared for the test is necessary to combat anxiety, but what does being prepared look like? You may study for hours on end and still not feel prepared. What you need is a strategy for test prep. The next few pages outline our recommended steps to help you plan out and conquer the challenge of preparation.

Step 1: Scope Out the Test

Learn everything you can about the format (multiple choice, essay, etc.) and what will be on the test. Gather any study materials, course outlines, or sample exams that may be available. Not only will this help you to prepare, but knowing what to expect can help to alleviate test anxiety.

Step 2: Map Out the Material

Look through the textbook or study guide and make note of how many chapters or sections it has. Then divide these over the time you have. For example, if a book has 15 chapters and you have five days to study, you need to cover three chapters each day. Even better, if you have the time, leave an extra day at the end for overall review after you have gone through the material in depth.

If time is limited, you may need to prioritize the material. Look through it and make note of which sections you think you already have a good grasp on, and which need review. While you are studying, skim quickly through the familiar sections and take more time on the challenging parts.

Write out your plan so you don't get lost as you go. Having a written plan also helps you feel more in control of the study, so anxiety is less likely to arise from feeling overwhelmed at the amount to cover.

Step 3: Gather Your Tools

Decide what study method works best for you. Do you prefer to highlight in the book as you study and then go back over the highlighted portions? Or do you type out notes of the important information? Or is it helpful to make flashcards that you can carry with you? Assemble the pens, index cards, highlighters, post-it notes, and any other materials you may need so you won't be distracted by getting up to find things while you study.

If you're having a hard time retaining the information or organizing your notes, experiment with different methods. For example, try color-coding by subject with colored pens, highlighters, or post-it notes. If you learn better by hearing, try recording yourself reading your notes so you can listen while in the car, working out, or simply sitting at your desk. Ask a friend to quiz you from your flashcards, or try teaching someone the material to solidify it in your mind.

Step 4: Create Your Environment

It's important to avoid distractions while you study. This includes both the obvious distractions like visitors and the subtle distractions like an uncomfortable chair (or a too-comfortable couch that makes you want to fall asleep). Set up the best study environment possible: good lighting and a comfortable work area. If background music helps you focus, you may want to turn it on, but otherwise keep the room quiet. If you are using a computer to take notes, be sure you don't have any other windows open, especially applications like social media, games, or anything else that could distract you. Silence your phone and turn off notifications. Be sure to keep water close by so you stay hydrated while you study (but avoid unhealthy drinks and snacks).

Also, take into account the best time of day to study. Are you freshest first thing in the morning? Try to set aside some time then to work through the material. Is your mind clearer in the afternoon or evening? Schedule your study session then. Another method is to study at the same time of day that you will take the test, so that your brain gets used to working on the material at that time and will be ready to focus at test time.

Step 5: Study!

Once you have done all the study preparation, it's time to settle into the actual studying. Sit down, take a few moments to settle your mind so you can focus, and begin to follow your study plan. Don't give in to distractions or let yourself procrastinate. This is your time to prepare so you'll be ready to fearlessly approach the test. Make the most of the time and stay focused.

Of course, you don't want to burn out. If you study too long you may find that you're not retaining the information very well. Take regular study breaks. For example, taking five minutes out of every hour to walk briskly, breathing deeply and swinging your arms, can help your mind stay fresh.

As you get to the end of each chapter or section, it's a good idea to do a quick review. Remind yourself of what you learned and work on any difficult parts. When you feel that you've mastered the material, move on to the next part. At the end of your study session, briefly skim through your notes again.

But while review is helpful, cramming last minute is NOT. If at all possible, work ahead so that you won't need to fit all your study into the last day. Cramming overloads your brain with more information than it can process and retain, and your tired mind may struggle to recall even previously learned information when it is overwhelmed with last-minute study. Also, the urgent nature of cramming and the stress placed on your brain contribute to anxiety. You'll be more likely to go to the test feeling unprepared and having trouble thinking clearly.

So don't cram, and don't stay up late before the test, even just to review your notes at a leisurely pace. Your brain needs rest more than it needs to go over the information again. In fact, plan to finish your studies by noon or early afternoon the day before the test. Give your brain the rest of the day to relax or focus on other things, and get a good night's sleep. Then you will be fresh for the test and better able to recall what you've studied.

Step 6: Take a Practice Test

Many courses offer sample tests, either online or in the study materials. This is an excellent resource to check whether you have mastered the material, as well as to prepare for the test format and environment.

Check the test format ahead of time: the number of questions, the type (multiple choice, free response, etc.), and the time limit. Then create a plan for working through them. For example, if you have 30 minutes to take a 60-question test, your limit is 30 seconds per question. Spend less time on the questions you know well so that you can take more time on the difficult ones.

If you have time to take several practice tests, take the first one open book, with no time limit. Work through the questions at your own pace and make sure you fully understand them. Gradually work up to taking a test under test conditions: sit at a desk with all study materials put away and set a timer. Pace yourself to make sure you finish the test with time to spare and go back to check your answers if you have time.

After each test, check your answers. On the questions you missed, be sure you understand why you missed them. Did you misread the question (tests can use tricky wording)? Did you forget the information? Or was it something you hadn't learned? Go back and study any shaky areas that the practice tests reveal.

Taking these tests not only helps with your grade, but also aids in combating test anxiety. If you're already used to the test conditions, you're less likely to worry about it, and working through tests until you're scoring well gives you a confidence boost. Go through the practice tests until you feel comfortable, and then you can go into the test knowing that you're ready for it.

Test Tips

On test day, you should be confident, knowing that you've prepared well and are ready to answer the questions. But aside from preparation, there are several test day strategies you can employ to maximize your performance.

First, as stated before, get a good night's sleep the night before the test (and for several nights before that, if possible). Go into the test with a fresh, alert mind rather than staying up late to study.

Try not to change too much about your normal routine on the day of the test. It's important to eat a nutritious breakfast, but if you normally don't eat breakfast at all, consider eating just a protein bar. If you're a coffee drinker, go ahead and have your normal coffee. Just make sure you time it so that the caffeine doesn't wear off right in the middle of your test. Avoid sugary beverages, and drink enough water to stay hydrated but not so much that you need a restroom break 10 minutes into the test. If your test isn't first thing in the morning, consider going for a walk or doing a light workout before the test to get your blood flowing.

Allow yourself enough time to get ready, and leave for the test with plenty of time to spare so you won't have the anxiety of scrambling to arrive in time. Another reason to be early is to select a good seat. It's helpful to sit away from doors and windows, which can be distracting. Find a good seat, get out your supplies, and settle your mind before the test begins.

When the test begins, start by going over the instructions carefully, even if you already know what to expect. Make sure you avoid any careless mistakes by following the directions.

Then begin working through the questions, pacing yourself as you've practiced. If you're not sure on an answer, don't spend too much time on it, and don't let it shake your confidence. Either skip it and come back later, or eliminate as many wrong answers as possible and guess among the remaining ones. Don't dwell on these questions as you continue—put them out of your mind and focus on what lies ahead.

Be sure to read all of the answer choices, even if you're sure the first one is the right answer. Sometimes you'll find a better one if you keep reading. But don't second-guess yourself if you do immediately know the answer. Your gut instinct is usually right. Don't let test anxiety rob you of the information you know.

If you have time at the end of the test (and if the test format allows), go back and review your answers. Be cautious about changing any, since your first instinct tends to be correct, but make sure you didn't misread any of the questions or accidentally mark the wrong answer choice. Look over any you skipped and make an educated guess.

At the end, leave the test feeling confident. You've done your best, so don't waste time worrying about your performance or wishing you could change anything. Instead, celebrate the successful completion of this test. And finally, use this test to learn how to deal with anxiety even better next time.

Review Video: Test Anxiety
Visit mometrix.com/academy and enter code: 100340

Important Qualification

Not all anxiety is created equal. If your test anxiety is causing major issues in your life beyond the classroom or testing center, or if you are experiencing troubling physical symptoms related to your anxiety, it may be a sign of a serious physiological or psychological condition. If this sounds like your situation, we strongly encourage you to seek professional help.

Online Resources

Due to our efforts to try to keep this book to a manageable length, we've created a link that will give you access to all of your online resources:

mometrix.com/resources719/nesincmusic

It's Your Moment, Let's Celebrate It!

Share your story @mometrixtestpreparation